Hardy's Early Poetry

*To Ginny —
A Thousand Thanks
for a thousand-and-one
favors — Jim*

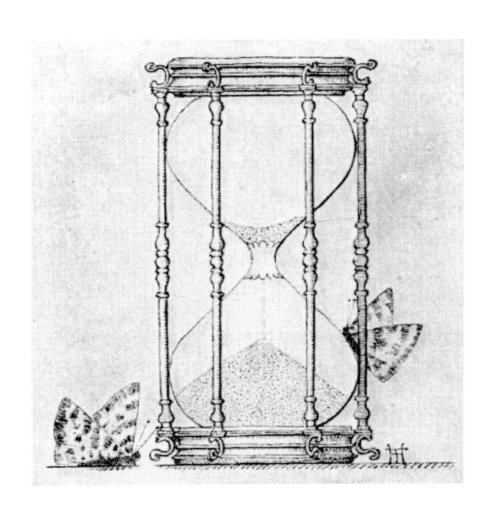

Hardy's illustration for "Amabel" in *Wessex Poems*

Hardy's Early Poetry

Romanticism through a "Dark Bilberry Eye"

James Persoon

LEXINGTON BOOKS
Lanham • Boulder • New York • Oxford

LEXINGTON BOOKS

Published in the United States of America
by Lexington Books
4720 Boston Way, Lanham, Maryland 20706

12 Hid's Copse Road
Cumnor Hill, Oxford OX2 9JJ, England

Copyright © 2000 by Lexington Books

The four illustrations reprinted in this book are original drawings by Thomas Hardy and are taken from his collection *Wessex Poems* (New York: Harper & Brothers, 1898).

All rights reserved. No part of this publication may be reproduced, stored in a retrieval system, or transmitted in any form or by any means, electronic, mechanical, photocopying, recording, or otherwise, without the prior permission of the publisher.

British Library Cataloguing in Publication Information Available

Library of Congress Cataloging-in-Publication Data

Persoon, James, 1950–
    Hardy's early poetry : romanticism through a "dark bilberry eye" / James Persoon
      p. cm.
    Includes bibliographical references (p.) and index.
    ISBN 0-7391-0152-8 (cloth : alk. paper)
    1. Hardy, Thomas, 1840–1928—Poetic works. 2. Polarity in literature.
3. Doubles in literature. I. Title.

PR4757.P58 P47   2000
821'.8—dc21   00-036226

Printed in the United States of America

∞™ The paper used in this publication meets the minimum requirements of American National Standard for Information Sciences—Permanence of Paper for Printed Library Materials, ANSI/NISO Z39.48–1992.

Contents

Preface		vii
Introduction		1
Chapter 1	Hardy's Empirical Ghosts	5
Chapter 2	Poems of the 1860s: The Division of the Universe	17
Chapter 3	Poems of the 1860s: The Otherness of the Female	37
Chapter 4	Hardy's Double Vision of Language	47
Chapter 5	Hardy and Metaphor	63
Chapter 6	The Question of Hardy's Development	79
Appendix	Hardy's Mentors and Kinships	93
Bibliography		101
Index		107
About the Author		111

Preface

"I'm from Iowa. It took me a long time to realize we were free to leave."—Jake Johansson

I came to know Thomas Hardy's work rather late, not until almost my thirties, but I immediately identified with it, through several thematic similarities in our early lives: a rural, backwater upbringing, in which literariness was alien; an aspiration to the religious life, dashed by a loss of faith; a sense of having one's feet in two worlds, the childhood one of local dialects and accents and the educated one of the university; a longing for return to the past twinned with a desire to escape to something better; a preoccupation with love experienced mostly at a distance or in the imagination, perhaps consisting of no more than a smile in the lane. Though better educated than Hardy in terms of diplomas, I am not at all as well-read as he managed to be. After studying Hardy now for two decades, I am continually surprised by him. Though I initially read all of the *Complete Poems* one summer nearly twenty years ago (with a doggedness perhaps familiar to Hardy in his own studies), I keep "seeing" poems I have never seen before. I can appreciate Philip Larkin's pleasure in the size of the *Complete Poems*; I often dip in at random, knowing that fresh surprises await me. For these reasons, I think, writing about Hardy feels personally important to me.

But writing about Hardy also leads me to feel out of my depth. The best critical minds of our era have been preoccupied with him at some time or another, and certainly most of the poets have taken note of him. All that I can take comfort in is that my own idiosyncratic mode of regard, if only in some accidentally felicitous phrasing, will open up a poem or a thought some afternoon in a library for a reader who dips into the right page of this study. Just as Hardy felt himself a young man until fifty, I feel very young in this enterprise, a student still and not a professor. And yet my own teachers, whom I thought would always be there, have mostly retired or passed away. I can no longer thank some of them: Albert Walker, my first Shakespeare professor; Donald Benson, who taught me Milton and Dryden; Stephen Goldman, who taught me linguistics; Thomas O'Donnell, who first led me to the modern British and Irish poets. As always, I thank those who are still here: Peter Casagrande, who first taught me Hardy; Roy Gridley, who helped me to love the Brownings; John McCully, who passed on to me his passion for the Middle Ages; David Mutchler, Girbe Eefsting, and Robert Bly, who have taught me what I know about Jung and Freud; Karl Gwiasda, who still teaches me about the Victorians; and my colleagues Alan Shucard, Rob Watson, and Patricia Hagen, who read parts of this work. Special thanks goes to the steadfast Ginny Klingenberg, whose cheerful persistence unravelled some of the more arcane problems of Windows and Word, and to librarians R.N.R. Peers and Don Pady. I also remain grateful for my family, those who are here and those who are no longer here, but especially my father, Leo Persoon, who is now eighty-six and looking uncannily like Hardy in his old age, and my brother Jerome (1961-1999), whose humor, like Hardy's, was swift, ironic, and delightful to those privileged to know him.

Introduction

"There was a portrait of Hardy . . . that melancholy, rapt, remarkable, small, secret face."—Edward Blishen

"Nobody who comes from a spell of reading in Hardy's poetry," David Daiches once wrote, "can have the slightest doubt he has been living with a deeply pessimistic imagination. No amount of analysis in the study can alter this central fact."[1] Fresh from another spell of living with Hardy's imagination, I am forced to agree and yet not agree. I am reminded of the lines of Archilochus, "the fox knows many things, but the hedgehog knows one big thing," which Isaiah Berlin used as a way to classify writers. For Berlin, Tolstoy was a fox who wanted to be a hedgehog. For me, Hardy is a hedgehog who pretends to be a fox. His poetry abounds with a clever variety and freshness of forms, situations, language, and ideas ("musings," he would no doubt prefer), but he hedgehog-like holds fast to a central truth about things that is unshakeable. That central truth I am tempted to call his "vision," an important word for Hardy and for Hardy criticism.

Hardy's "vision," as so many critics have recognized, is split. We all have different names for it and use different metaphors to describe it: double vision, bi-focaled vision, dualism, a vision of dualities or binary oppositions. For J. Hillis Miller, the split was between twin poles of detachment and engagement, distance and desire; for Harold Bloom, Hardy made Shelley into a mentor who, like Hardy, was "a visionary skeptic, whose head and whose heart could never be reconciled, for they both told truths, but contrary truths"; Tom Paulin saw in Hardy "a passive empiricism and an active idealism"; over forty years ago Samuel Hynes called it an "antinomial tension between his thoughts and his feelings"; almost sixty years ago John Crowe Ransom called it "honey and gall"; my teacher Peter Casagrande saw it as "a dreamy wish to have things as they had been and a hardheaded conviction that—except imaginatively—they could never be so"; a graduate student friend many years ago, Judith Thompson at the University of Kansas, remarked that in writing about Hardy, she was, as with Yeats, always writing "and yet"; Robert Langbaum has recently written that "for an atheistic realist Hardy populates his poems with a surprising number of ghosts," an implicit dualism that stands as the epigraph for my first chapter; and Isobel Armstrong argues that the "belatedness" or secondariness which the Victorians were conscious of in relation to their great predecessors resulted in "the double poem, with its systematically ambiguous language, out of which expressive and phenomenological readings emerge."[2] Laurence Lerner reminds us that the word *vision* itself contains a dualism: "vision is what your oculist treats, and it is what the mystic experiences, it means both what comes through the eye and what transcends ordinary sight."[3] Perhaps it is redundant, then, for me to refer to Hardy's "double vision" in this study, but my metaphor of the two eyes, one realistic and one romantic, is meant to make the inherent duality more transparent.

Hardy in actuality did have two different-appearing eyes. This fact comes to us from Sir William Rothenstein, who painted Hardy: "He remarked on the expression of the eyes in the drawing I made—he knew the look, he said, for he was often taken for a detective. He had a small dark bilberry eye which he cocked at you unexpectedly."[4] The "bilberry eye" has the cold gaze of a detective looking for a hard fact out of which to solve a mystery: the dark, empirical eye scrutinizing the material world while the other, "visionary" eye concerns itself with the mystery of the transcendent world. One cannot make much more of this fact, perhaps, but it would have pleased the Hardy who liked to defend such apt coincidences with "it really happened!"

To note that so many critics have found so many dualities in Hardy is of course not surprising, nor is it unique to Hardy, for we live in a civilization which pervasively makes such categorical distinctions: male and female, life and death, day and night, good and evil, and so on.[5] As Jonathon Culler noted long ago, one can always find some aspect in which two items differ and hence place them in a relation of binary opposition. So Hardy's "dualism" may in fact be one's own dualistic imagination. Rather than enter into that ultimately circular debate, let me turn to the pieces of Hardy's vision most visible to me. In each of the following chapters, I will focus on a work, usually a single poem, to illustrate that chapter's concerns. Chapter 1 centers on "A Sign-Seeker" as a way to look at the empiricism which determines Hardy's way of knowing about the world. Chapter 2 examines how Hardy may be seen to divide the world into opposite and irreconcilable parts, using the earliest poems as evidence; "Her Dilemma" summarizes the dilemmas which Hardy's double vision creates for him. Chapter 3 traces how Hardy perceives male and female as another duality, so that the female stands, not surprisingly, as "other" for him, but also stands for us in our "otherness" in the universe; the "She, to Him" sonnet sequence is central to this chapter. Chapter 4 turns to language, Hardy's single support in the world against alienation, his one way to abandon the passive, watchful stance and speak publicly to his fellow human beings. Insofar as his view is the Lockean one, that language is a closed system in which with careful enough definitions one can build up truth from a small, empirically tested base, Hardy is imprisoned in the categories that his empiricism creates. And yet the language itself, older than the new sciences, contains other, teleological features that contradict the categories of mechanism and the antimetaphysical metaphysics which Hardy has asked his language to carry; central to this chapter is Hardy's essay "Memories of Church Restoration." Chapter 5 looks at a particular language feature, metaphor, and focuses on Hardy's own sometimes escape from the mechanical world his empiricism creates. This escape is made possible by the imaginative creation of an opening in the inherited metaphor of the universe as a prison. Chapter 6 returns to the early poems, especially "Neutral Tones," to examine the question of Hardy's development as a poet.

Notes

1. David Daiches, *Some Late Victorian Attitudes* (New York: Norton, 1969), 71.

2. J. Hillis Miller, *Thomas Hardy: Distance and Desire* (Cambridge: Harvard University Press, 1970); Harold Bloom, *A Map of Misreading* (Oxford: Oxford University Press, 1975), 22; Tom Paulin, *Thomas Hardy: The Poetry of Perception* (Totowa, N.J.: Rowman & Littlefield, 1975), 193; Samuel Hynes, *The Pattern of Hardy's Poetry* (Chapel Hill: University of North Carolina Press, 1956), 45; John Crowe Ransom, "Honey and Gall," *Southern Review* 6 (1940), 5; Peter J. Casagrande, *Unity in Hardy's Novels* (Lawrence: Regents Press of Kansas, 1982), 59; Robert Langbaum, *Thomas Hardy in Our Time* (London: Macmillan, 1995), 30; Isobel Armstrong, *Victorian Poetry: Poetry, Poetics, Politics* (London: Routledge, 1993), 16.

3. Laurence Lerner, "Moments of Vision—and After," in *Celebrating Thomas Hardy*, ed. Charles P. C. Pettit (London: Macmillan, 1996), 24.

4. *Men and Memories: Recollections of William Rothenstein, 1872-1900* (New York: Coward-McCann, 1931), 303.

5. The categories *day and night* and *good and evil* have long admitted to "gray" areas, but increasingly we are seeing how some other formerly rigid dualities have broken down. *Life and death* has become problematical with medical advances that allow the body to remain "alive" while the brain is "dead," and the hermaphrodites' rights movement has similarly deconstructed

male and female. For more on the latter, see Alice Dreger's *Hermaphrodites and the Medical Invention of Sex* (Harvard: Harvard University Press, 1998), which argues that it was Victorian anxieties about gender-blurring that led the medical profession to decide at birth that a child was one of two genders, and Thomas Laqueur's *Making Sex: Body and Gender from the Greeks to Freud* (Harvard: Harvard University Press, 1992), which describes how historically male and female bodies were viewed not as distinct but as existing on a continuum from imperfect (female) to perfect (male).

Chapter 1

Hardy's Empirical Ghosts

> "For an atheistic realist Hardy populates his poems with a surprising number of ghosts"—Robert Langbaum, *Thomas Hardy in Our Time*

Hardy's "philosophy" has from the first been a standard topic in criticism. This has usually meant that his famous pessimism has somehow to be accounted for, leading us to negotiate between his lifelong claim that he had never held a consistent philosophy and the evidence of his careful reading of Darwin, Hume, Mill, Spencer, Schopenhauer, and Comte, among others. In the larger context of the nineteenth century, Hardy does not necessarily appear more pessimistic than his contemporaries, if one looks beyond the poets. Ruskin said he could not read the Bible without hearing the clink of the geologist's hammer; Mill had to remind himself that a cloud could be beautiful even though he knew that it was really only vapors in a state of suspension; and Darwin himself complained that he could no longer enjoy reading *Paradise Lost*, which had been his mainstay during the voyage of the *Beagle*. What makes Hardy unusual is that, with his awareness of the new sciences of geology, biology, and positivist philosophy, he chose to be a poet. His strict insistence on empirical truth, however, separated him from the transcendental views of even the most doubtful of nineteenth-century poets.

Tom Paulin's early book *The Poetry of Perception* (1975) is built upon examining Hardy's empiricism, what the "despotism of the eye" meant for him. While I will not re-cover that ground, I would like to approach Hardy's empiricism, but along a slightly different path. Rather than examine the heritage of Locke, Newton, Bentham, and Mill, I want to begin with Hardy's own peculiarly strong and lifelong interest in ghosts, both as literal presences and metaphoric imaginings of something beyond the literal. Understanding what ghosts meant for Hardy is one way of understanding his poetry, which is so frequently haunted by them.

Hardy's autobiography (itself ghostwritten in that he directed it to be published by his second wife, Florence, as her own work) gives ample testimony to his lifelong interest in spectres as a doorway to the past. One ghost from the past he avidly sought, through pilgrimages in England and Italy, was his beloved Shelley. In 1879, on meeting his favorite poet's son, also named Percy Shelley, Hardy remarked (in his third-person description of himself) that the meeting was as shadowy and remote as were "those previous occasions when he had impinged on the penumbra of the poet he loved. . . . He was to enter that faint penumbra twice more, once when he stood beside Shelley's dust in the English cemetery at Rome, and last when by Mary Shelley's grave at Bournemouth" (*Early Life*, 171-72). The haunting, however, did not have to be by anyone with the lingering fame of a Shelley, or even by a person, as this note on a scene revisited after an absence of eighteen years shows: "Went to Hatfield. Changed since my early visit. A youth thought the altered highway had always run as it did. Pied rabbits in the Park, descendants of those I knew. . . . I regretted that the beautiful sunset did not occur in a place of no reminiscences, that I might have enjoyed it without their tinge" (*Early Life*, 72-73). Thus past highways, and even rabbits, could dominate a present scene, and, characteristically, impinge on present happiness. Equally implicated are the unnamed reminiscences. In Robert Langbaum's phrase from *Thomas Hardy in Our Time* (1995), Hardy perpetually suffers from the "psychological ghosts of Wordsworthian involuntary memory" (30). More recently, Tim Armstrong has named the elegiac tradition, as practiced by Hardy, as "the place where the ghost of the literary past is addressed."[1] Hardy is unable, in the face of his "[p]ied rabbits," to resist an involuntary elegizing of their ghostly fathers.

Objects of all sorts brought the past to life for Hardy. When he takes a furnished house, the worst of it for him is that "the articles in the rooms are saturated with the thoughts and glances of others" (*Later Years*, 17-18). On walks through the country, he is helpless to keep from seeing Wordsworthian underpresences: "In spite of myself I cannot help noticing countenances and tempers in objects of scenery, e.g. trees, hills, houses" (*Later Years*, 58). Even time partakes of some unusual extra dimensions: "To-day has length, breadth, thickness, colour, smell, voice" (*Later Years*, 58). The saturation of objects with life, the investing of the present with echoes of the past, the inspiriting of the nonhuman world with human qualities through such devices as personifying abstractions like Time, these are some of the commonest motifs in his poetry.

Beyond even these en-ghostings, it was quite easy, and apparently habitual, for Hardy to imagine himself in the role of a ghost as well. In 1888 he met again Anne Thackeray (now Lady Ritchie), whom he had known through visits to Leslie Stephen's house in London in 1874. They talked of "the value of life," and she admitted that her interest in the future lay largely in the fact that she now had children. This conversation set Hardy on a train of thought that ended with this often-quoted note "a day or two later": "For my part, if there is any way of getting a melancholy satisfaction out of life it lies in dying, so to speak, before one is out of the flesh; by which I mean putting on the manners of ghosts, wandering in their haunts, and taking their views of surrounding things" (*Early Life*, 275). This is so, he continues, because "to think of life as passing away is a sadness; to think of it as past is at least tolerable. Hence even when I enter into a room to pay a simple morning call I have unconsciously the habit of regarding the scene as if I were a spectre not solid enough to influence my environment."

Hardy's preference for the past, as less sad than the constantly passing present, seems less strange when one realizes that by inhabiting a ghostly form Hardy has just created for himself what he otherwise consistently denies—an afterlife. He has found a way to let consciousness continue beyond death, for in the very sentence in which he imagines life as past, he continues to be able to watch the earthly scene and comment upon life's tolerableness. This is one value of ghosts for him, the solution they represent in salving the sadness of mortality.

This solution, though Hardy continues to flirt with it throughout his life, is never really convincing to him, for he repeatedly comes back to the problem of what the good of consciousness is if it all ends at death. Less than a year after his confession of "putting on the manners of ghosts," Hardy is again defining the predicament in which the human race finds itself: "A woeful fact—that the human race is too extremely developed for its corporeal conditions, the nerves being evolved to an activity abnormal in such an environment" (*Early Life*, 285). Hardy questions whether Nature "or what we call Nature, so far back as when she crossed the line from invertebrates to vertebrates, did not exceed her mission. This planet does not supply the materials for happiness to higher existences" (*Early Life*, 286). That is, the human race has too much mind for its body, too much mind to fit it comfortably in a material world. Hardy's argument is structured similarly to that of a speaker in a monologue by his friend Browning. This monologue, "Cleon," Hardy had imitated in "In St. Paul's a While Ago," a poem which in J. O. Bailey's phrase "subtly satirizes the prevalence of classic-pagan features in a Christian church" (511).

"Cleon" and "A Sign-Seeker"

Browning's Cleon, a late-classical poet-philosopher, replies to a letter from King Protus, who has asked the poet if he fears death less than other men, since a poet's life "stays in the poems men shall sing" while a king's dies with his "brain and arm" (ll. 170, 173). Cleon's answer is no. Like Hardy, he examines man's evolutionary progress: "Why stay we on the earth unless to grow?" (l. 114). And like Hardy, he concludes that evolutionary growth is ultimately Nature's mistake. Arguing that the great evolution ultimately amounts to nothing, Cleon answers Protus bitterly:

> Thou diest while I survive?
> Say rather that my fate is deadlier still,
> In this, that every day my sense of joy
> Grows more acute, my soul (intensified
> By power and insight) more enlarged, more keen;
> While every day my hairs fall more and more,
> My hand shakes, and the heavy years increase.
> (ll. 308-14)

The growth of one's faculties leads finally to the disappointment of death, a disappointment made only worse by the increase in power and insight. Cleon, significantly, seeks visible evidence: "—where is the sign? I ask,/And get no answer" (ll. 268-69). He gets no answer, he concludes, because "Zeus has not yet revealed it" (l. 334). Browning ends his poem ironically, with Cleon, who desires a revelation to prove that death is not final, in the last line dismissing certain barbarians, Paulus and Christus, whose "doctrine could be held by no sane man" (l. 353).

Hardy's poem "A Sign-Seeker," published some forty years after "Cleon," is usually seen as a response to Tennyson, not Browning. There are often-noted echoes in thought and phrasing to *In Memoriam*, while the rhyme scheme and even the printing of the lines recall that poem. In addition, "Locksley Hall" evidences more than a coincidental number of verbal echoes: *clanging, dipped, leaped, throngs of men, strife, night, shadows, phantoms, whisper, star, rise, scope, weigh the sun*. Hardy appears to be employing a Tennysonian vocabulary and form to dispute *In Memoriam*'s central argument.

Because the links to Tennyson are so clear, the ways in which Browning also stands behind Hardy's poem have not been noticed. In "A Sign-Seeker" Hardy places his speaker in the position of Cleon, looking for some visible sign of something beyond this life. As Tom Paulin remarks, each of the first five stanzas of the poem begins with an act of perception:

> I mark the months in liveries dank and dry,
>   The noontides many-shaped and hued;
>   I see the nightfall shades subtrude,
> And hear the monotonous hours clang negligently by.
>
> I view the evening bonfires of the sun
>   On hills where morning rains have hissed;
>   The eyeless countenance of the mist
> Pallidly rising when the summer droughts are done.
>
> I have seen the lightning-blade, the leaping star,
>   The cauldrons of the sea in storm,
>   Have felt the earthquake's lifting arm,
> And trodden where abysmal fires and snow-cones are.
>
> I learn to prophesy the hid eclipse,
>   The coming of eccentric orbs;
>   To mete the dust the sky absorbs,
> To weigh the sun, and fix the hour each planet dips.
>
> I witness fellow earth-men surge and strive;
>   Assemblies meet, and throb, and part;
>   Death's sudden finger, sorrow's smart;
> —All the vast various moils that mean a world alive.

In these first stanzas the world is imaged forth as an incredibly alive place of Darwinian, pre-Edenic beauty, vital yet unconscious, with a hint of danger—one can almost see the stage direction in some prehistoric monster movie cueing the "earth-men" to "surge and strive." Against a backdrop of "evening bonfires of the sun," planets dip, stars leap, rains hiss, mists rise, the earthquake lifts its arm. Into this chaotically alive world science intrudes to try to impose an order: "weigh the sun, and fix the hour each planet dips."

In subsequent stanzas of "A Sign-Seeker" what the speaker most wants sight of is not "all the vast various moils that mean a world alive" but rather "[t]hose sights of which old prophets tell,/Those signs the general word so well." Not trusting the words of the general mob, Hardy wants further

> To glimpse a phantom parent, friend,
>   Wearing his smile, and "Not the end!"
> Outbreathing softly: that were blest enlightenment.

In Hardy's brand of churchy agnosticism,[2] enlightenment is "blest" when it comes not from the revelation of the prophets but rather from optical proofs (here, a phantom) through which the ultimate chaos of dying is contradicted. Phantoms, however, have already entered this poem earlier, in the second stanza, where the mist, imaged with an "eyeless countenance," suggests the blind face of the spirit presences in the world, forecasting the unlikeliness of proving transcendence through visual proofs.

In the last stanzas of "A Sign-Seeker," Hardy most explicitly denies that eyes, as blank as the face of the mist, can find a proof for immortality. He does so in words strongly reminiscent of *In Memoriam*:

>—There are who, rapt to heights of trancelike trust,
>   These tokens claim to feel and see,
>   Read radiant hints of times to be—
> Of heart to heart returning after dust to dust.

Physical signs—seeing the face, feeling the pressure of a hand—are, in Hardy's reading, the foundations for Tennyson's trust in something better "which is to be" (*In Memoriam*, CXVI). In his 1875 copy of *In Memoriam* (its markings typographically reprinted by Dennis Taylor in the *Thomas Hardy Journal*) Hardy marked two lines containing images of touch: "The dead man touch'd me from the past" and "I take the pressure of thine hand." Hardy mocks the realness of any touch Tennyson might have felt by asking that any "dead Love" of his "leave some print to prove her spirit-kisses real." Hardy's "heart to heart returning after dust to dust" parodies Tennyson's stanza CXVI, "the life re-orient out of dust." Earlier in his poem he has given us a different vision of what becomes of dust, when the speaker says he has learned "to mete the dust the sky absorbs." Rather than the dust of a woman reorienting into some new life, dust here is measured as it is absorbed into the sky, and the measurement does not reveal Hardy's sky to be Tennyson's Heaven. The dust rising is reminiscent of the blank mist "[p]allidly rising," not to an afterlife but rather for a reason explainable in purely pragmatic terms: "the summer droughts are done."

Hardy rejects his Tennysonian stanza, however, with a line that owes more to Browning in its colloquialness and inversion: "Such scope is granted not to lives like mine." There is a faint echo here of the argument of *The Ring and the Book*, that art will yield truth, "to mouths like mine" (XII, 840). "For," as Browning asks, "how else know we save by worth of word?" (I, 828). Browning's book will "mean beyond the facts," even "suffice the eye" (XII, 862, 863). But for Hardy, the eye is not satisfied by visions nor the ear by language. There is no meaning beyond the facts, and the facts are grim:

> I have lain in dead men's beds, have walked
> The tombs of those with whom I had talked,
> Called many a gone and goodly one to shape a sign,
>
> And panted for response. But none replies;
> No warnings loom, nor whisperings
> To open out my limitings,
> And Nescience mutely muses: When a man falls he lies.

Nescience, a word not common to many poetic vocabularies, was a part of Browning's. He used it in "La Saisaiz," to a quite different purpose than Hardy, momentarily reforging a belief in God and soul[3]:

> Living here means nescience simply: 'tis next
>   life that helps to learn.
> Shut those eyes, next life will open. (ll. 469-70)

Where Browning images the possibility that when our eyes shut the next life opens, Hardy, unwilling to shut his eyes, panting for response, confronts Nescience, which does not "open out" his limitations, or the limits of the physical world. The personification is characteristically his, occupying the same place as God, who to Hardy was another personification. Hardy, like Cleon, seeks a sign, and receiving none, ends his poem with Cleon's doctrine of death. Cleon's "I . . . sleep in my urn. It is so horrible" is not very far from Hardy's "when a man falls he lies." That is knowledge to face up to.

In a patronizing comment about Browning, Hardy praised his own courage in facing up to this knowledge: "Imagine you have to walk [a] chalk line drawn across an open down. Browning walked it, knowing no more. But a yard to the left of the same line the down is cut by a vertical cliff five hundred feet deep. I know it is there, but walk the line just the same."[4] Again the issue of vision is crucial. Browning's vision, in at least religious matters, was to Hardy as narrowly limited as that chalk line.

The Primacy of Seeing

Despite his certainty in dismissing what he read in Browning as optimism, Hardy was never skeptical when it came to the possibility of actually sighting a ghost. His photographer-friend and motoring-companion Hermann Lea was emphatic on this point: "Very often this subject cropped up between us, for we were both interested—as who is not?—in the Great Future... He was always sympathetic and free from scepticism" (*Through the Camera's Eye*, 30). In a conversation with William Archer, Hardy made the offer to give up ten years of his life "to see a ghost—an authentic, indubitable spectre" (*Real Conversations*, 45). This was not an isolated wish. By Hardy's later years its wording had become as formulaic as a litany, as here recalled again by Lea: "Once, I remember, we dwelt on the subject of spiritualism and the possibilities of individuals 'seeing ghosts,' and I recollect him saying to me, 'I have always wanted to see a ghost: I am receptive and by no means sceptical. I would willingly concede ten years of my life if I could see any supernatural thing that could be proved to me to exist by any means within my capacity'" (30). The "capacity" through which Hardy would allow proof that a ghost was "authentic" and "indubitable" is of course the chief organ of the previous century's empiricists, sight, its mechanics adumbrated by Newton's *Opticks*, its relation to the mind and the ability to know developed by Locke's *An Essay Concerning Human Understanding*, its place above all the other senses praised by Addison's *Spectator 411*.

This emphasis on sight as final proof of transcendence is evident in Hardy's most direct formulation on the subject of the ultimate purpose of life: "I have been looking for God for 50 years, and I think that if he had existed I should have discovered him. As an external personality of course—the only true meaning of the word" (*Early Life*, 293). As Purdy notes, Hardy in these later years refused to capitalize pronouns referring to God, although, interestingly enough, *God* itself he wrote in the standard way—another balancing act between denial and belief for the churchy yet agnostic Hardy. Hardy has been "looking"; he's always wanted "to see" a ghost, or, here, God, or even just the oxen kneeling on Christmas eve—some "sign." A question one might ask is why he so insisted on seeing a ghost when any reader of his poetry or listener to his conversation or eavesdropper on his private thoughts in his autobiography would everywhere find him "seeing" ghosts: in houses with faces, trees with voices, days with smells, rabbits with ghostly ancestors, in the imprint of long-dead worshippers in church pews and stone steps, of hands on thresholds and stair-railings, of fingers that once played the strings of a violin, of his wife Emma's shadow in their garden and in other scenes he revisited after her death. Why this insistence on literally seeing a ghost when, metaphorically speaking, ghosts were obviously and everywhere visible to Hardy?

One is forced to conclude, I believe, from the strictness of his formulations on the subject, that, for Hardy, sight was not only the best but ultimately the only way of knowing about something as deeply important as an afterlife. If this is true, the poems of the past (and present) whereby he "gives life" to a dead person by remembering her or him have then a frightening literalness to them. Only the empirically alive have life, can give life, or take life. And by extension, only poetry which stays in print has life or "reality." This casts a different light on the admirable clause in Hardy's will that his poetry always be in print and at a price affordable to a common workingman. As much as we see his concern for the poor Judes of this world who have the talents but not the means for advancement, we also see a man determined "to leave some print to prove . . . [his] spirit kisses real." If, as the next chapter hopes to demonstrate, Hardy saw the world in terms of acute polarizations between irreconcilable opposites—"antinomies"—then ghosts take on another importance. They point out the boundary line in Hardy's division of the world, a line running sharply between empiricism and romanticism. As reputed visitants to this world from the next, ghosts have a unique ability to bridge the gap between the two worlds. In addition, because ghosts are invisible but also "seen," they allow for empirical proof of something transcendent. This in part answers why throughout his life Hardy was so eager and ready to see a ghost. To possess a literal sign of transcendence would be to possess the most intensely wished for and perpetually unlocatable quality in Hardy's universe, and prove life *not* a "trick of Nature on the vertebrates."

Though Hardy never got a sign to his satisfaction, one eye was always firmly fixed on the place where heaven was supposed to be. The insistence that heaven be a place and that God be a personality left heaven and God unproved and Hardy unconvinced, and ensured that "A Sign-Seeker" would end with the attitude of Cleon rather than with the irony of Browning.

This insistence on the primacy of the literal vision of a ghost over the imaginative one so pervasive in his writings seems to fly in the face of so much else of what Hardy was about—to name just one example, the epigraph to *Jude the Obscure*, "the letter killeth." If the letter of the law, the literal, "killeth," but yet is the final reality, how do we value the literal? How the figurative? How do we value imaginative work such as poetry if the figurative is less "real" than the literal? The literal has primacy and the literal kills. There is a tremendous tension for a poet here, a tension which manifests itself in Hardy as a kind of split vision of the world. This split vision is implicit in Hardy saying, "I have always wanted to see a ghost." His transcendentalist side, inherited from his parents, his religion, his Romantic forebearers, wants a belief in an afterlife. But his empirical side, an outgrowth of two centuries of the scientific revolution, insists on a positivist proof before allowing for such a belief. This dualism is implicit from the start, in Hardy's earliest poems.

A final word about dualisms. If deconstructionist theory has shown us nothing else, it has clearly demonstrated that dualities can always be shown to deconstruct each other.[5] What such a deconstruction of the poles of Hardy's universe would show us would be the conflicting ideologies of science and religion, and that Hardy's "science" was really a religion, and his "religion" actually science. But this we already know. The nineteenth century itself understood that these two important ways of knowing were in conflict. In fact, the introduction to Browning in one of Hardy's marked-up copies at the Dorset County Museum even treats the matter as a commonplace, naming the conflict the struggle between "religion and scientific criticism" or between "Faith and Doubt." Similarly, other dualisms that one might wish to explore—male and female, for example—will likewise reveal the conflicted ideologies of the times. Exploring dualisms in Hardy's poetry will not create a system of consistent philosophy for him nor will it show that any reading of his poetry is untenable, but it may allow us to try to "sit on the fence" with Hardy, in Tom Paulin's phrase, and notice what there is to see from that slightly elevated if unstable perch.

Notes

1. See Tim Armstrong's "Year's Work in Victorian Poetry" in *Victorian Poetry* 37 (1999), 339.

2. See Evelyn Hardy's *Thomas Hardy: A Critical Biography* (New York: Russell & Russell, 1954), 306: "Since both men lived during an age of transition, when fresh scientific discoveries were being made and were casting religious tenets into doubt, both Donne and Hardy revealed the aching need for a faith wherewith to confirm themselves. Donne transferred his religious allegiance from one church to another and so, in part, consoled himself. Hardy was unable to do this. Yet even he, avowed agnostic, often attended services, and when walking to Stinsford churchyard declared: 'I believe in going to church. It is a moral drill, and people must have something.'"

3. See Roy Gridley's *The Brownings and France: A Chronicle with Commentary* (London: Athalone Press, 1982), 286-89, for a discussion of Browning's attempt in "La Saisaiz" to "unravel any tangle of the chain" of his recent experience of death in the Haute-Savoie.

4. Quoted by Michael Millgate in *Thomas Hardy: A Biography* (Oxford: Oxford University Press, 1976), 409.

5. See Shirley A. Stave's *The Decline of the Goddess: Nature, Culture, and Women in Thomas Hardy's Fiction* (London: Greenwood Press, 1995), 2 ff., for a fuller discussion of the perils of negotiating critical theories, both feminist and deconstructionist, when looking at this charged subject matter.

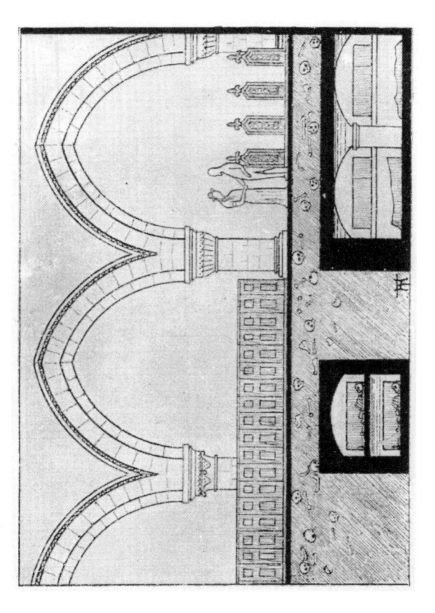

Hardy's illustration for "Her Dilemma" in *Wessex Poems*

Chapter 2

Poems of the 1860s: The Division of the Universe

> "There is a peculiar agony in the paradox that truth has two forms, each of them indisputable, yet each antagonistic to the other."—Edmund Gosse, *Father and Son*

To speak of the poems of the 1860s raises a prior issue, that is, the dating of Hardy's poetry, which is always a difficult enterprise.[1] This is primarily because the evidence we have is in the form of manuscript "fair" copies, rather than the original manuscripts, which Hardy regularly destroyed. Additionally, the motives for the destruction of the originals are not clear. The simplest explanation is that Hardy wrote and revised so much that rudimentary housekeeping demanded occasional purges of paper. Another explanation is that, once his poems were in print, Hardy, like many writers, felt his children were raised and sent out into the world. Though he continued to pay attention to their reception and refinements, he no longer needed their red-faced baby pictures. Of course, many parents and many writers are sentimental about the awkward beginnings of their progeny and nostalgically hold onto those first scrawls and wails, which would seem more characteristic for the notoriously nostalgic Hardy. And then there is Hardy's demonstrated willingness to mislead us, especially in matters of privacy and self-protection, as in his secretly self-penned official biography. From his sensitivity to critics and criticism, one might posit that less-than-fluent beginnings of poems would invite destruction or concealment. It is against this background that Hardy's dating of "Domicilium" as his earliest effort, written in 1857-1860, has been seriously challenged, by Peter Casagrande and others who have questioned whether Hardy may not have been choosing to construct for himself a Wordsworthian beginning as most fitting to give out to his public.[2]

If one accepts Hardy's dating, the earliest poems after "Domicilium" come from the years 1865-1867, at the end of his five-year sojourn in London working for the architect Arthur Blomfield. Sixteen of the twenty-eight poems which Hardy dated as coming from this time are to be found in his first published volume of poetry, *Wessex Poems* (1898): "Amabel," "Hap," "In Vision I Roamed," "At a Bridal," "Postponement," "A Confession to a Friend in Trouble," "Neutral Tones," "Her Dilemma," "Revulsion," "She, to Him I," "She, to Him II," "She, to Him III," "She, to Him IV," "The Bride-Night Fire," "The Two Men," and "Heiress and Architect."[3] The rest of the poems of the 1860s are scattered among Hardy's later volumes. Two appear in *Poems of the Past and Present* (1901): "Her Reproach" and "The Ruined Maid"; seven in *Time's Laughingstocks* (1909): "1967," "Her Definition," "From Her in the Country," "Her Confession," "To an Impersonator of Rosalind," "To an Actress," and "A Young Man's Epigram on Existence"; two in *Late Lyrics and Earlier* (1922): "A Young Man's Exhortation" and "Dream of the City Shopwoman"; and one in *Human Shows* (1925): "Discouragement." The themes of these early poems explore Hardy's relationships to Nature, to God, and to other men and women. While he was to grow in skill beyond these early poems, the main lines of his thinking emerge in them full-blown, if one looks at vision rather than theme. That vision shows from the first a fierce dualism. It is Hardy's true religion.

In Hardy's view of the world there are two strands: an objective external reality and a subjective human consciousness. They coexist but do not complement one another. The second has arisen from the first; that is, human consciousness has arisen evolutionarily from an unconscious world and is thus both alien to that world and yet a part of it. This is Nature's trick on the vertebrates. Consciousness (or, as Hardy says in the famous passage from 1889, quoted in the last chapter, "nerves") is alien to this planet, more properly fitted for another, and yet also a part of this planet, evolved from it.[4] This view of unreconciliable duality was not Hardy's unique conception, but rather a common notion among those who had lived through the crises of the 1860s produced by Darwin's *The Origin of Species*. The epigraph to this chapter, by Hardy's friend the novelist and critic Edmund Gosse, comes from Gosse's 1907 autobiography, in which Gosse describes his father, a zoologist who knew Darwin personally, unsuccessfully attempting to reconcile fundamentalist Christian faith with the powerful vision science was formulating. Gosse's father ultimately turned his back on the truths of evolutionary theory, ingeniously arguing that, at the moment of creation, fossils and other evidences of gradualism and mutability had been simultaneously created. Hardy's solution to the challenge which science offered religion in the 1860s was to lose his faith but write poems embodying the conflict.

Hardy's sense of the incompatability of human consciousness and the world finds early expression in the poems of 1865-1867 as a vision of dualities. People in the early poems are creatures who feel, but learn that feeling is an emotion confined to the space of their own bodies; the external world is not set up to respond to their peculiar ability to feel. People have another faculty, reason, which tells them this truth of the world's indifference to them. These two faculties, the ability to feel and the ability to reason, gain expression in the poems as visions, romantic and realistic.[5] When the romantic eye is turned full-focus, the result is an idealization, the creation of a golden and transcendent world out of the materials which the vision falls upon. When the realistic eye is brought into focus, idealizations vanish. The figurative constructions built by the romantic eye turn back into literal pieces of an objective, external reality.

The early poems offer examples of both extremes. For pure idealization there is the sonnet "Her Definition," in which the lovesick poet labors through the night to find an epithet that might "outfigure" his love, but by the end of the octect can think of only three inadequate words: "That maiden mine!" The sestet, however, redeems this inadequacy and lifts the poem's speaker into flights of extravagance:

> As common chests encasing wares of price
> Are borne with tenderness through halls of state,
> For what they cover, so the poor device
> Of homely wording I could tolerate,
> Knowing its unadornment held as freight
> The sweetest image outside Paradise.

It could be argued that the marvelous overstatement of these last six lines has more to do with a long sonnet tradition of extravagant praise for one's love than with any vision peculiar to Hardy. Certainly "To an Actress" and "To an Impersonator of Rosalind" support that argument. Both are early sonnets and both idealize women whom Hardy, from all evidence, observed only as a member of an audience (Bailey, 221). But Hardy saved thirteen other sonnets from the 1865-1867 period, none of which is fully given over to the idealizing vision. Sonnet convention, then, is not the cause of the vision; Hardy was more versatile than that.

The other extreme also occurs in the early poems. The counterpart of the lover's extravagant praise in "Her Definition" is the lover's wish in "1967," a poem which looks at love a century hence. The one poem's praise of the beloved as the "sweetest image outside Paradise" is reduced in "1967" to the wish that after a century "thy worm should be my worm, Love!" This shocking image of lovers united by a single worm feeding on both corpses is an example in which a figurative, romanticized construction—"the sweetest image outside Paradise"—is turned back into a literal and nontranscendent image. The figure of Paradise gives way to the visible worm.

"Her Definition" and "1967" are companion pieces in a section of *Time's Laughingstocks* (1909) titled, somewhat ironically, "More Love Lyrics." This section, which includes the idealizing "To an Impersonator of Rosalind" and "To an Actress," concludes with "He Abjures Love," in which the narrator, "too many times ablaze/With fatuous fires," abjures not so much love as the romanticizing tendency:

> No more will now rate I
>   The common rare,
> The midnight drizzle dew,
>   The gray hour golden,
> The wind a yearning cry,
>   The faulty fair,
> Things dreamt, of comelier hue
>   Than things beholden!

Gray replaces golden, faulty replaces fair, dew changes to drizzle. By virtue of being named first, drizzle and gray are given a status of existence which Hardy does not allow to dew and golden. The poem suggests that there never was a real dew for Hardy's speaker to see. The definite article is attached to "drizzle," so that the definite substance is drizzle at midnight, which the speaker in the past has fatuously mistaken for dew. In the same way, the hour, in reality, is gray; the speaker once rated it golden. That earlier romantic rating has lost any reality it previously held for the speaker. The romantic eye is now, by the last two lines, the eye asleep, the eye dreaming. It has in fact ceased to be an eye altogether, for now all things beheld belong to the speaker's new mode of seeing.

The disappointed lover has not only sworn off the romanticizing eye; he has given a new rating or ranking to the relative value of his two ways of seeing. "Things dreamt" are no longer comelier than "things beholden." That is, the romanticized vision, fair, golden, and rare, is no longer the more beautiful. At this point a reader may wonder whether Hardy's speaker is asserting that the dream is unbeautiful, or that the realistic is equally beautiful to the romantic. Has all the incredible beauty of the romantic vision now been transferred to the realistic, or is there now no beauty to be seen at all, or has a new, terrible beauty been born?

Behold things as they are, the speaker exclaims. Yet what wondrous things are we to behold? Drizzle. Grayness. The faulty. A wind no longer instinct with sympathetic Wordsworthian life but just a common wind. It is difficult to feel the wonder which the act of beholding suggests is in these things, difficult to find the beauty which resides in these things equal to the beauty of that rare, fair, golden dew. Hardy, in short, is careful that in the realistic vision beauty drops out. We are left with a real tension. The beautiful is fictive. The real is unbeautiful. Take your pick, truth or beauty, but know that both are flawed because each excludes the other.

The poem's ending leaves no doubt that the beauty one sees while in love has disappeared. The narrator speaks as

> One who at length can sound Clear views and certain.
> But—after Love what comes?
>   A scene that lours,
> A few sad vacant hours,
>   And then, the Curtain.

The stage curtain ending life's few sad vacant hours is the final image of reality in this poem, as reductive as the worm in "1967." Insofar as Hardy's phrasing calls to mind "Tintern Abbey" and the "Immortality Ode," which Hardy frequently echoes in his poetry, it is anti-Wordsworthian. The melancholy of the "still sad music of humanity" and of the "hour/Of splendour in the grass" is made beautiful for Wordsworth by the knowledge of the permanence of a "primal sympathy." For Wordsworth, the mind of man and Nature are interfused, completing each other as a part of the same creation. For Hardy, mind and nature are quite separate and uncomplementary. The realistic vision, when employed full focus, as in these two poems, sees death. The linking of *curtain* and *certain* by rhyme and curtain's final position in the poem suggest the certainty and finality of death. Moreover, the final position of this poem in "More Love Lyrics" strongly suggests the characteristic relationship of the two modes of vision in Hardy's work. Final place (and with it, primacy) is given to the more certain of the two visions—a dead reality, or the reality of death—rather than the less visible, less literal, less certain transcendence of, here, love.

The Fence-Sitter's Dilemma

Tom Paulin in a succinct image calls Hardy a fence-sitter who "lean[s] towards the positivists' camp while preferring to defect in the other direction" (44). Here Hardy does more than lean toward the positivists; he falls off the fence at poem's end, over to their side altogether. But Hardy's most characteristic posture in the early poems is the fence-sitter. I take "Her Dilemma" as a central poem among the 1865-1867 lyrics, showing Hardy's dual vision in all its characteristic complexity.

> The two were silent in a sunless church,
> Whose mildewed walls, uneven paving stones,
> And wasted carvings passed antique research;
> And nothing broke the clock's dull monotones.
>
> Leaning against a wormy poppy-head,
> So wan and worn that he could scarcely stand,
> —For he was soon to die—he softly said,
> "Tell me you love me!"—holding long her hand.
>
> She would have given a world to breathe "yes" truly,
> So much his life seemed hanging on her mind,
> And hence she lied, her heart persuaded thoroughly
> 'Twas worth her soul to be a moment kind.
>
> But the sad need thereof, his nearing death,
> So mocked humanity that she shamed to prize
> A world conditioned thus, or care for breath
> Where Nature such dilemmas could devise.

Here a woman is asked by a man about to die to say she loves him. Her dilemma is that she values truth and kindness equally highly, but is forced to choose one and turn her back on the other. She chooses kindness. Her dilemma is created, the poem says, by the condition of the world. What is that condition? The world she moves in is figured in this poem as a church, the traditional repository of the transcendent vision. This church, however, is not golden, but sunless. It does not fit her, but is uneven. It is not alive with transcendent meaning but rather quite depressingly physical and dying: the carvings are "wasted," the poppy-head "wormy," the walls "mildewed." The chief sound in the church is mechanical, the monotones of the clock. In short, the world figured by this church is the empiricist one quite alien and separate from the life of human consciousness. It is a world wherein it is not possible to do the best that the human mind can imagine. The "world conditioned thus" is in its most fundamental sense a world in which we must die. Against this fact, "to care for breath" is short-sighted, hence foolish, and hence shaming. Nature takes one's breath moment by moment, and death is always near at hand. Hardy's drawing accompanying this poem shows the close presence of death, underneath the couple's feet. The process of dying is evident in the various states of decay shown in the tombs. The church, founded on the triumph of the cross over death, seems here to be built on a foundation of skulls. In fact, there is not a cross in the drawing; all that appears from the Crucifixion story is the reminder of Golgotha, the "place of skulls." The Gothic arches in this picture have no heaven to point to, or at most, the space allowed for heaven is small and empty. Death, representing both the past and the future, is certainly far more prominent. The woman's understanding of death's presence makes it absurd to care for his breath or for hers.

There is a second and more important reason the woman is shamed to "care for breath/Where Nature such dilemmas could devise." The world is not worth caring about because it is alien from the human and unable to respond to caring. It is less in its reality than the human can imagine and yet more powerful than the human. The world is thus cruel, and it is shaming to prize a cruel life, which at best is still a too great falling off from what the human imagination desires. Thus the world is conditioned two ways. First, it is dead; second, as a result of this first condition, it devises cruel dilemmas for creatures who must live in it but are alive with feeling.

Her attempt to create a solution is interesting: "She would have given a world to breathe 'yes' truly" and "'Twas worth her soul to be a moment kind." These are quite appropriate choices: trading a world to be able to choose truth, trading her soul to be able to choose kindness. In Hardy's religion, truth belongs to the world-rational, scientific, empirical, material. *Kindness* belongs to the human-emotive, imaginative, fictive, alive with spiritual possibility. In this schemata, the human being by his or her nature chooses kindness. But at the same time that Hardy forces his heroine to choose, he deconstructs his rigid dualities, for she is also, obviously, of the world, and thus also values truth. The dilemma has expanded by the final stanza. It is not only whether to choose truth or kindness, but whether to choose one part of oneself over another; whether to value reason or human feeling; whether to see the world as it truly is or to see in it what should be; whether to lose all that is beautiful and valuable but be in harmony with the universe or to be foolish but capture some of the beautiful. What makes these dualities into a paradox is that neither choice is a real alternative. One cannot forget what one knows or forget what one values.

"Her Dilemma" is a paradox in a box. Once one steps into the box of Hardy's universe, its rules prevent happiness and prevent escape. The same dilemma confronts Hardy's most famous heroine, Tess, and for her Hardy has to invent a word in "Tess's Lament": "I'd have my life unbe."

More common formulations for one gripped by despair would be "I wish I were dead" or "I wish I'd never been born!" But Tess recognizes Nature's dilemma. She cannot opt out by death; death is a part of Nature, the Nature which does not care for human happiness, and her death will cause pain to the fellow creatures she leaves behind. To be out of Nature's trap she must not only *not* exist, but also *not have* existed. To say, "I wish I'd never been born" or "I wish I'd never existed," while the proper sentiment for escape, still gives her an existence, an "I" who wishes. The most neutral formulation Hardy can find for erasing existence is in that small word "unbe," as simple and deadly as the modern *delete* key.

One could proceed through the early poems arranging them on a scale, according to which vision is most in focus. When the realistic is operating without the idealizing vision, the result is a detached, often cosmic, perspective. "Hap" is the best-known example. In "Hap," Chance and Time, the major forces in the cosmos, are indifferent to man. Their detached indifference is set out as an explanation for why "joy lies slain." "Amabel" offers a similar perspective on beauty and love. From the perspective of time passing, beauty is temporary, and with beauty's fading so fades love.

Hardy's illustration accompanying "Amabel" shows an hourglass almost empty, a symbol for time and life passing. The two butterflies in the drawing suggest beauty, but a fragile and ephemeral beauty from the viewpoint of any longer-lived creature. In Christian art butterflies can represent the transformed soul leaving the body, and thus in this poem would show a kind of permanence surviving death and time, which is also suggested by "the Last Trump" of the poem, calling souls to judgment. It is always problematical in Hardy, however, to know how one is to take traditional Christian allusions. If read as an image of the soul, the butterflies add a leavening of transcendence to this account of love fading. The poem, however, ends on a rather casual note of farewell rather than a solemn promise to meet again at the Last Judgment:

> But leave her to her fate,
> And fling across the gate,
> "Till the Last Trump, farewell,
>   O Amabel!"

Additionally, the possible gaming metaphor in "Last Trump" ties "Amabel" to the world of "Hap" more than to the Christian scheme. Paul Turner's *The Life of Thomas Hardy* (1998), which frequently provides a reading of the classical allusions in Hardy, suggests that "Amabel" comes from Hardy's knowledge of Horace's ode to "a lady whom

Horace had wrongly thought *semper amabilem* (always to be loved)" (163). If that is so, there may also be a pre-Christian iconography of butterflies which Hardy knew from his study of the classics and of which I am unaware. The butterflies are important, however, for what they reveal about matters of scale. Without them, "Amabel" remains on the human scale of time. With the reminder of the butterflies, we are nudged toward a larger perspective. We are lifted to a cosmic perspective by reflecting upon the microcosmic perspective of their lives, lived on the scale of time represented by an hourglass. If "Hap" shows us a detached realism by reaching for a telescope, "Amabel" achieves the same effect by having us examine the smaller life nearer to our notice.

"In Vision I Roamed" jumps back up to the stars, showing us a traveller roaming the "flashing Firmament" whose spirit ranges "[I]n footless traverse through ghast heights of sky,/To the last chambers of the monstrous Dome,/Where stars the brightest here are lost to the eye." "Ghast," "monstrous," and "brightest" indicate the immensity of the traveller's new perspective. The next line of this sonnet returns us to Earth, where, after a glimpse of the flashing universe, "any spot . . . seemed home!" The cosmic perspective, however, is still maintained, though domesticated, in the sestet:

> And the sick grief that you were far away
> Grew pleasant thankfulness that you were near,
> Who might have been, set on some foreign Sphere,
> Less than a Want to me, as day by day
> I lived unware, uncaring all that lay
> Locked in that Universe taciturn and drear.

The speaker's lover, who before his musings in this poem seemed far away, seems finally near, in the sense that any spot on Earth where she might be seems near compared to other spheres.

This poem is usually read as showing the unimportance of man in a "taciturn and drear" universe.[6] Read this way, it is much like "Hap" and a good example of Hardy's empiricism dominating a poem. That reading can be deepened by paying closer attention to the final two lines. The universe in the poem is figured spatially as a container, room, or box, with chambers, dome, heights, and a lock. It is a dreary, uncommunicative ("taciturn") box, and, in the words of the poem, an "uncaring" box. The adjective "uncaring" can also be read as referring to the speaker: "I lived unware, uncaring [about] all that lay/Locked in that Universe." The speaker thus achieves an identity with the Universe. Both are, by the syntax of the poem, uncaring. "Unware" now takes on additional meaning. This is not just a poem about a speaker comforting his "sick grief" at separation by imagining the potentially greater grief of living in an uncaring universe and being unaware of his lover's existence. In our expanded reading, "unware" means "unconscious." We can become as unconscious and as uncaring as the universe. A person without love, or "unware" of love, becomes unware/unconscious, as dead a thing as that box of a universe he or she is locked in. Without love to excite such emotions as "sick grief," we become an unconscious, uncaring piece of an unconscious, uncaring universe. Thus even while emphasizing the nonhuman qualities of the universe we live in, this poem also elevates love as the essential human quality.

This nonhuman or antihuman quality of the universe is again described in "Discouragement." It is not only humankind that is buffeted about by the larger forces of the universe. Even Mother Nature, planning to "mint a perfect mould" and "don divinest hues," is dismayed and defiled by an unfaithful and more powerful lord; just as her "plans for bloom and beauty [are] marred," so the lives of her creatures are determined by this same lord, who seems to rule by whim or chance:

> . . . loves dependent on a feature's trim,
> A whole life's circumstance on hap of birth,
> A soul's direction on a body's whim,
> Eternal Heaven upon a day of Earth.

In each case, the accident of feature, birth, or whim takes precedence over love, life, or the soul. The realism of the Earth is given rule over the values of Heaven. In the last line of this sonnet we are told that this dominance by the realistic is "fosterer of visions ghast and grim." The realistic vision in Hardy is the grim vision. If his poetry is grim, we might hear Hardy say, so is the truth. All that can be opposed to this truth is an ethic of "loving-kindness" ("Apology" to *Late Lyrics and Earlier*). This opposition, remember, is the same that was offered in "Her Dilemma."

A Vision of Loving Kindness

We have looked at the early poems in which Hardy's "realistic" vision operates most powerfully. Let us turn to those among the early poems in which the vision of "loving-kindness" most strongly asserts itself.

We have already seen that when the romantic vision is operating without the realistic, the result is such pure idealizations as "Her Definition," "To an Actress," and "To an Impersonator of Rosalind." Let us look at the latter poem, because it has an interesting companion, "The

Two Rosalinds," written several decades later but published in the same volume with the earlier poem. In the first of the Rosalind poems, the 1867 sonnet, the speaker imagines Shakespeare with the foreknowledge to discern what perfect actress would one day be playing the role he was writing, so that when his lines are spoken all men can agree that because of her "fairnesses" this is the "'very, very Rosalind' indeed!" In "The Two Rosalinds," the speaker returns after forty years to again see "a Rosalind woo and plead,/On whose transcendent figuring my speedy soul had centered/ As it had been she indeed." He is disappointed in the new Rosalind, however; as he leaves the theater he finds that the "hag" outside hawking the words to the play is indeed the very Rosalind of the original transcendent moment, and so the speaker must face a double disillusionment. Time has caused both, the same time which ruined Amabel and is here, in the third poem of *Time's Laughingstocks*, responsible for preventing the playgoer from "seeing what I once had seen."

By not publishing the early sonnet until he had written "The Two Rosalinds," and then publishing both in the same volume, Hardy effectively undercut one of the few pure examples of the romantic vision to be found among all the poems. In the rest of the early poems, it is within the poem itself that Hardy undercuts the romantic vision. "A Young Man's Exhortation" seems at first not to follow this pattern. In this poem, not published until *Late Lyrics and Earlier* (1922), the speaker exhorts "call off your eyes from care," "put forth joys," "exalt. . . the hour/That girdles us," and "[s]end up such touching strains/That limitless recruits from Fancy's pack/Shall rush upon your tongue." The exhortation is necessary, the speaker says,

> For what do we know best?
> That a fresh love-leaf crumpled soon will dry,
> And that men moment after moment die,
>   Of all scope dispossest.

Against this knowledge of death, of the short hour within whose girdle we act, the speaker asserts the surpassing preciousness of the imagination:

> If I have seen one thing
> It is the passing preciousness of dreams;
> That aspects are within us; and who seems
>   Most Kingly is the King.

Unlike Amabel and the revisited Rosalind, who are ruled by time, this speaker claims not to be ruled by the world without; for him it is the aspects within that rule.

In manuscript, according to Purdy (218), this poem was titled, "An Exhortation." By renaming this a *young* man's exhortation, Hardy introduces some irony into the last stanza. When a *young* man says, "If I have seen one thing," one wonders just how much he has seen. In his conclusion that "who seems/Most Kingly is the King," one wonders about living for the appearance of things as they are in the present. Time may well change that "seems." A further irony is introduced by the pun in "passing." Clearly the young man means the word to say that dreams pass all other preciousnesses, but the older man has to be aware of how difficult it is to "call off . . . [one's] eyes from care" all for the sake of a "passing preciousness."

If the last two stanzas were reversed, this would become a more typical Hardy poem, much like "He Abjures Love," or "1967," or "The Two Men," ending with one's consciousness of death as the final reality. Hardy does not make that change; he leaves this as a celebration of romantic assertion overriding the knowledge of human frailty and mortality. But he does, by changing the title, make sure we know that this poem is a young man's exhortation, not the view of a poet in his eighties.

Its humor makes the well-known "Ruined Maid" seem another exception to Hardy's typical care to undercut the romantic vision. But the lightness of the poem is darkened by its sequel, "A Daughter Returns." Bailey suggests that after reading over "The Ruined Maid," published November 17, 1901, Hardy wrote the sequel, which is dated December 17, 1901. The outraged father of the second poem pictures his own suffering:

> When the cold sneer of dawn follows night-shadows black as
>   a hearse,
> And the rain filters down the fruit tree,
>
> And the tempest mouths into the flue-top a word like a curse,
> Then, then I shall think, think of thee!

Even if the poem is read as a satire on the father, the good-humored banter of the first has changed here to a curse, and the picture of country life has become tempestuous and sneering, cold and filled with images of death.

In "Dream of the City Shopwoman" and "From Her in the Country" the romantic vision asserts itself in the beginning of the poems as a protagonist's faith in happiness. Both the shopwoman and the girl in the country believe that happiness is attainable; it just happens to reside in a place somewhere other than their own. The shopwoman wishes for a cottage of thatch and clay to live a pastoral life (this is a fantasy acted out by Marie Antoinette at Versailles, where she dressed as a milkmaid and tended animals beside her elaborate cottage):

> Our clock should be the closing flowers,
> Our sprinkle-bath the passing showers,
> Our church the alleyed willow bowers.

The maid in the country wishes, of course, for the city. At first she tries to enjoy the country life:

> I said: How beautiful are these flowers, this wood,
> One little bud is far more sweet to me
> Than all man's urban shows; and then I stood
> Urging new zest for bird, and bush, and tree.

Hers is an admirable effort, but the humorously flat "for bird, and bush, and tree" signals the hollowness of the country for her. She gives up trying: "But it was vain; for I could not see worth/Enough around to charm a midge or a fly." The couplet ending this sonnet has the country lass musing again "on city din and sin,/Longing to madness I might move therein!" "From Her in the Country" remains a delicately humorous characterization, yet the "crass clanging town" and "city din and sin" which she madly desires seem equally as unlikely a source of happiness as her view of country life.

For the city shopwoman, the dream of country bliss ends abruptly when she herself introduces the realistic: "—But all is dream!" She utters a lament that recalls Hardy's exclamation in *The Dynasts*, "the intolerable antilogy of making figments feel," when she addresses God:

> O God, that creatures framed to feel
> A yearning nature's strong appeal
> Should writhe on this eternal wheel.

The image of sentient creatures writhing on a wheel, writhing precisely because they feel, is a statement of Hardy's tragic realism. The wheel as an image of the earth combines overtones of the rack, of the Newtonian world-machine, and of the medieval Wheel of Fortune which finally brings man back down to low estate and death after raising him up to temporary good fortune. This abrupt realism has been prepared for in the shopwoman's earlier images of pastoral bliss; the darker vision is implicit in the "closing" flowers, "passing" showers, and "willow" bowers.

Both "From Her in the Country" and "Dream of a City Shopwoman" begin with dreamy idealizations; both end with the intrusion of the realistic. That they were written in the same year suggests that Hardy meant them to be viewed as antidotes, each canceling out the other's romanticized notion of a happy life.

"Heiress and Architect" can serve as a paradigm for the kind of Hardy poem I have been describing. The heiress begins with the romantic notion of building a house open to nature, but the "archdesigner," wise in the ways of the grand design of things, reminds her that nature can be cruel. This poem has been seen as a debate between the romantic Wordsworthian dream and the realistic Darwinian fact, with fact winning out and the house bit by bit stripped down, in the end shrunken to a coffin.[7] In Hardy's drawing, the house which began with "tracery and open ogivework" and "wide fronts of crystal glass" is reduced to the eminently practical stairs wide enough to haul the coffin out when the occupant dies. The coffin bearers are rather startlingly faceless, heads cut off. They exist in outline only, Casper-the-ghost-like. Their awkwardly alive yet dismembered bodies carrying the coffin downstairs give a sense of the equally awkward disjointedness the heiress contends with in building the house, a sense, taught her by the architect, of prevailing death-in-life.

At this point we have examined fifteen of the twenty-eight early poems. Five of these—"Her Definition," "To an Actress," "To an Impersonator of Rosalind," "The Ruined Maid," and "A Young Man's Exhortation"—are given over to the romanticizing vision, and that vision is partially undercut in the last three. The scale would be further tipped toward the empiricists if we included the rest of the early poems. Some by their very titles indicate which vision is more at work, as for example "At a Bridal: Nature's Indifference," or "Neutral Tones."

The title of "Revulsion" seems to indicate the same realistic vision predominating. The speaker decides it would be better to fail obtaining a hypothetical love because the pain accompanying the loss of love is so certain and so keen:

> Though I waste watches framing words to fetter
> Some unknown spirit to mine in clasp and kiss
> Out of the night there looms a sense 'twere better
> To fail obtaining whom one fails to miss.

> For winning love we win the risk of losing,
> And losing love is as one's life were riven;
> It cuts like contumely and keen ill-using
> To cede what was superfluously qiven.

Out of this imaginative foreknowledge, the speaker vows never more to seek love:

> Let me then never feel the fateful thrilling
> That devastates the love-worn wooer's frame
> The hot ado of fevered hopes, the chilling
> That agonizes disappointed aim!
> So may I live no junctive law fulfilling
> And my heart's table bear no woman's name.

He rejects love out of hand, in the last two lines almost with a curse. The image of his "heart's table" seems rigid and rational, and has overtones of the Lockean *tabula rasa* and a tombstone. His contemplated rejection of love comes at great price; he must give up the thrilling and the hopes along with the chilling and the agonies. "Revulsion" is "Her Dilemma" with the protagonist making the other choice, choosing the truth of the world over the love of the human heart. One denies what she knows in order to do the kindness she wishes; the other denies what he wishes because of what he knows. The choice is different but the result is the same: the choice is unsatisfactory. By choosing to reject love, this speaker has not even avoided pain; he has just bought a different kind of pain.

"Revulsion," like "Her Dilemma," is best seen as neither realistic nor romantic, for the speakers in both poems are people caught in between: neither vision alone is wholly satisfactory and the visions are, sadly to Hardy's way of thinking, irreconcilable. A poem such as "Revulsion" shows just how far Hardy is from his contemporary Yeats, who after recognizing that "man . . . loves what vanishes," will still throw himself into that frog-spawn of a ditch called life a second time to love. Hardy's speaker goes half as far. He accepts that love will bring pain, but he also does not accept the pain. His state is revulsion—he is revolted, but he does not revolt. Neither is he resigned to passivity. He hangs between the romantic and the realistic, between revolution and resignation, in revulsion, without the freedom to leave the dilemma.

The poem Hardy chose to close *Time's Laughingstocks*, "A Young Man's Epigram on Existence," is another of the early poems which shows this quality:

> A senseless school, where we must live
> Our lives that we may learn to live!
> A dolt is he who memorizes
> Lessons that leave no time for prizes.

The message comes from Hardy's understanding of paradox in the world; but the epithet "senseless" and the exclamation point are pure protestation against that paradox. Hardy does not deny the truth of realism, nor does he resign himself to it, but neither does he triumph over it. "Her Dilemma" remains central, for the early poems replicate its dilemma: that in this world we are offered two compelling but opposing choices.

The Polarities of Hardy's Universe

From the early poems so far examined, a series of these choices has emerged. They can be tabulated in word pairs as the polarities of Hardy's universe:

Realistic	Romantic
Literal	Figurative
Material	Transcendental
Rational	Emotive
Time-Bound	Eternal
Change	Permanence
Law	Desire
Darwinian	Wordsworthian

One could expand this table of binary oppositions indefinitely, creating a rich soil for deconstructing terms. Some are immediately problematic, even in the often reductive descriptions of the poems in this chapter. For example, *Nature* is at times the indifferent force on the left-hand side of the chart and at other times the feeling Mother who mourns our marring. Does "She" go on the right-hand side then? Such a "chart-busting" move would reveal Hardy's (and the nineteenth century's) unease with the competing views of nature which Wordsworth and Darwin iconically represent.

Additionally, the pairings in this table look suspiciously like Helene Cixous's table of "the sexist binaries structuring Western patriarchal discourse," in Jan Montefiore's words (180). It is not hard to guess on which sides of the table *male/female* should be arrayed. And yet *female*, as we shall see, has a slippery placement in Hardy's universe, sometimes standing in for humankind in the same way that in traditional English *man* or *he* stands for all of humankind. Each of these polarities could be grounds for further study demonstrating exactly to what purposes Hardy used it. The next chapters, however, will examine only a few of these polarities in greater detail. The groundwork of polarities laid in this chapter would allow us to reexamine the opening chapter on ghosts by looking at what such oppositions as *literal/figurative* and *visible/invisible* meant for Hardy. This chapter has concentrated on *knowing/feeling* and *truth/kindness*, as well as detailing a longer list of dualities. The next chapter concerns itself with an opposition not yet in the table—*male/female*.

The table shows a series of choices. Given these choices, one is tempted not to make a choice at all, but to become a passive, detached observer (as in J. Hillis Miller's formulation) or a fence-sitter (as Tom Paulin phrases it), and indeed, this is what Hardy is famous for. But a life of watching, of passivity, is itself a choice, one of the dualities Hardy creates. The dualities listed here are an inescapable trap. If one divides up the universe as this series of choices suggests, there is literally no middle ground on which to rest. One is forced into choice, and choice can only be unsatisfactory. For example, which is one to prefer, truth or beauty? Given the necessity of choice, Hardy finally chooses the less desirable but more irresistible. His oft-alleged pessimism, one might argue, stems from his choice of the less desirable, and from his unwilling willingness to remain in that choice. One of Hardy's less than explicit statements on the matter shows this awareness: "Men endeavour to hold to a mathematical consistency in things, instead of recognizing that certain things may be both good and mutually antagonistic . . . [for example] unbelief and happiness" (*Later Years*, 54). The Architect in us, mirroring the cruel truths of the Great Architect, holds to a mathematical consistency, but the Heiress in us, heir to a Romantic past and a Heavenly throne, recognizes the importance of holding onto the mutually antagonistic qualities of life in this world.

Notes

1. Dennis Taylor, in "The Chronology of Hardy's Poetry," *Victorian Poetry* (spring 1999), 1-57 makes a detailed attempt to date the poems and place them into six stages showing Hardy's development. Taylor accepts rather uncritically, however, Hardy's dating of the earliest poems.

2. See Peter J. Casagrande, "Hardy's Wordsworth: A Record and a Commentary," *English Literature in Transition* 20 (1977), 212 for suggestions that "Domicilium" may not be an early poem, at least in its entirety. See Brian

Green, "The Composition and Publication of 'Domicilium,'" *Thomas Hardy Journal* (1993) 91-94 for an argument that the poem betrays evidence of the mature Hardy at work. See Kenneth Marsden, *The Poems of Thomas Hardy: A Critical Introduction* (New York: Oxford University Press, 1969), 181-210 for a discussion of Hardy's revisions and the warning that in the early poems "we are forced to deal with what has survived, and without any guarantee that it has survived unaltered."

3. *Wessex Poems* gives the impression of a haphazard collection, containing sonnets, ballads, and homemade stanzas, in various meters, some dated and some not, illustrated irregularly throughout with Hardy's own line drawings and concluding with five poems in a section called "Additions," almost as an afterthought. The volume is unified, according to Paul Zietlow, only by its vision, which is in the main dark, bleak, and negative, with a secondary melody of muted hopefulness. See *Moments of Vision* (Cambridge: Harvard University Press, 1974), 1-9. The volume received mixed reviews. It seemed a hodge-podge of undecipherable Sapphics, knockoffs of Shakespearean and Miltonic sonnets, quarrels with Tennyson and Wordsworth, Barnesian dialect pieces, and Kiplingesque ballads about the Napoleonic Wars, with a dash of Swinburne and Meridith added to the stew. But it did have its supporters, notably Meredith and Swinburne, and more recently John Lucas, who on the centennial of *Wessex Poems's* publication wrote an appreciative defense of its plan and its power for the *Thomas Hardy Journal*. The drawings which Hardy published with the poems are cited by Lucas as a unifying force in the volume and a sign of new energy and a new start, moving away from the fashionable end-of-century pose of decadence.

4. J. Hillis Miller's *Thomas Hardy: Distance and Desire* (Cambridge, MA: Harvard University Press, 1970), 12-13 describes the emergence of this dualism in Hardy's universe: "There is only one realm, that of matter in motion, but out of this 'unweeting' (*Dynasts, 99*) movement human consciousness, that 'mistake of God's' ("I Travel as a Phantom Now," *Complete Poems*, 429), has arisen accidentally, from the play of physical causes. Though the detached clarity of vision which is possible to the human mind has come from physical nature, it is radically different from its source. It sees nature for the first time as it is, has for the first time pity for animal and human suffering, and brings into the universe a desire that events should be logical or reasonable, a desire that people should get what they deserve. But of course the world does not correspond to this desire. This is seen as soon as the desire appears." A more contemporary description of this dualism can be seen in the 1907 autobiography of Hardy's friend, Edmund Gosse, who speaks of his father's dilemma as both a fundamentalist Christian and a professional zoologist who knew Darwin, Huxley, Lyell, et al., personally: "Through my Father's brain, in that year of scientific crisis, 1857, there rushed two kinds of thought, each absorbing, each convincing, yet totally irreconcilable . . . that there were two theories of physical life, each of which was true, but the truth of each incompatible with the truth of the other" (*Father and Son*).

5. Other names that critics have used for *romantic* are *transcendent, imaginative, Platonic, spiritual-sacramental,* and *mystic*; for *realistic*, critics

have used *empiricist, rationalist, materialist, utilitarian, positivist*. None of these names is totally without potential for confusion and ambiguity. This problem is discussed at length by Wendell V. Harris, *The Omnipresent Debate* (DeKalb: Northern Illinois University Press, 1981), 3-20, who cautions that so long as the terms one chooses (his choices are *transcendentalism* and *empiricism*) are understood to designate "the polar halves of a mental compass" rather than to name specific philosophical doctrines, they provide "a kind of intellectual orientation that is otherwise difficult to achieve among the strong currents and countercurrents of nineteenth-century English thought" (11).

6. Bailey, *The Poetry of Thomas Hardy*, 53; Kenneth Marsden, *The Poems of Thomas Hardy* (New York: Oxford University Press, 1969), 53; Ross C. Murfin, *Swinburne, Hardy, Lawrence and the Burden of Belief* (Chicago: University of Chicago Press, 1978), 89.

7. Paulin identifies the architect with Newton, science, empiricism, and Bentham, while the heiress is the other extreme, of "romantic idealism" (36). See also Bailey, *The Poetry of Thomas Hardy*, 108. Hardy's use of Wordsworth and Darwin is discussed in Roger Robinson, "Hardy and Darwin," in *Thomas Hardy: The Writer and His Background* ed. Norman Page (London: Bell and Hyman, 1980), 128-150, and in Roger Ebbatson's chapter "Hardy: The Complete Darwinian" from his *The Evolutionary Self* (New Jersey: Barnes & Noble, 1982).

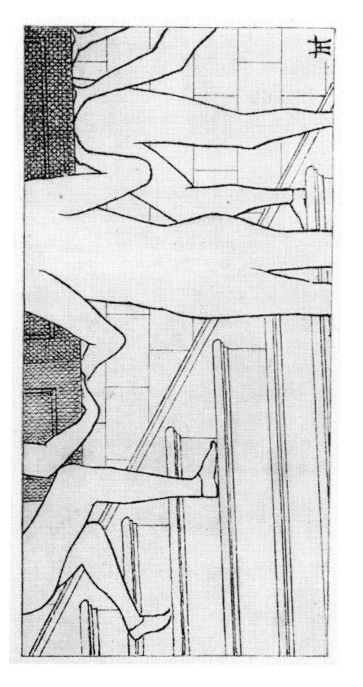

Hardy's illustration for "Heiress and Architect" in *Wessex Poems*

Chapter 3

Poems of the 1860s: The Otherness of the Female

"Any girl can be glamorous. All you have to do is stand still and look stupid."—Hedy Lamarr

The most widely praised of Hardy's early poems, "Neutral Tones," drains color, love, and life from the world with a completeness that takes in the death of all nature. The universe of the poem is reminiscent of the boxlike, insentient universe imaged in "In Vision I Roamed," in which humans are an anomaly. In the six of the early poems dated 1867 still to be examined (the four "She, to Him" sonnets; "Her Reproach"; "Her Confession") the same universe obtains, but the speakers of these poems do not make what in the rest of the early poems is the irresistible choice.

These speakers are all women in love.[1] Each of them insists on the transcendent power of her love. When they come to realize that their love relationships are temporary, they do not reject the ideal of love, but rather value it even more intensely. The women of these poems are constant and single-minded in their passion as none of the male personae of the early poems ever are. The woman of "She, to Him III" proclaims "I will be faithful to thee; aye, I will!" Her ringing double "I" in the first line, tripled by the homophonic "aye," implies a more powerful will to assert love in the face of death than any man in the early poems will allow himself to muster. There is no question in her mind whether the ecstasy of love is worth the pain that accompanies loss; she does not even need to ask herself that question in the poem; her faith stands for her as a given. With more reason than the speaker of "Revulsion" to reject love (for he, after all, is imagining a hypothetical future pain) she, after a "last Good-bye," is incapable of his rejection of love. Rather, she stays as constant and true as a weather vane cankered on its point.

Whether this is a mechanical image of a metal vane rusting into a frozen position or an organic image of a wooden vane decaying into constancy, the vane suffers deterioration. The canker/cancer is thus an image of both deterioration and constancy. As an image, the canker reminds us that this woman is asserting her constancy in full knowledge of the decay of love. She is not ignorant, like the Dorsetshire farmworker who will be happiest longest on earth because he will be ignorant the longest of the real conditions of human existence ("The Dorsetshire Labourer," in Orel, 169). She asserts love with full knowledge of love's end. Time enters this poem when the speaker forecasts her "old dexterities in witchery gone/And nothing left for Love to look upon." This is "Amabel" from another perspective, the female and the romantic. Rather than asserting that with the fading of beauty love must fade, this poem shows love unfading while still on earth despite time's ravages. Hers is, however, quite clearly a grim and one-sided love.

This preservation of love against the force of time is closely akin to a common theme in Hardy, the power of memory. The mind that remembers has a power to preserve life. In "Her Immortality" from *Wessex Poems* Hardy treats this theme quite explicitly: the speaker visits the place where last he saw his love alive, and in a trance she comes to him to explain that

> A Shade but in its mindful ones
>   Has immortality;
> By living, me you keep alive,
>   By dying you slay me.

The successful preservation by memory is rare, as a poem such as "Ah, Are You Digging on My Grave?" shows. This well-known poem has the same kind of decremental structure as "Heiress and Architect," with the dead woman guessing who it is who remembers her and finding each hope of faithful remembrance stripped away, as it is not her lover, nor kin, nor even enemy who has come to her grave. She learns finally that it is her dog, who also does not remember her but was only carrying on with his doggy life by burying a bone against future hunger. The woman's belief in the permanence of affections is destroyed by the knowledge that she is dead in a second way. Carried in the minds of the living, she has a kind of spiritual life, a ghostly habitation of the present.

This existence-in-memory, however, has still a very visible, physical side to it—the memory must be that of a still-living person. In "Her Immortality," when the rememberer dies, so does memory: "By dying you slay me." Hardy does not in this poem give to memory a verifiable, independent status. Memory, too, like all else that belongs to the transcendent vision, needs to be yoked to the physical world, because Hardy allows only the empirical vision to verify what is "real." When memory or love can no longer be yoked to the physical world, the woman who relies on memory or love finds her position undercut. Physical death ends both. Empiricism this way wins its victory over transcendence. The mind that remembers is moral. Its power, however, is temporary and incomplete. Memory preserves only until the death of the rememberer. And memory preserves not the whole person and a living love but rather a phantom half-being and a mummified, static love. The mind which forgets, on the other hand, is disloyal, animal, and spiritually dead. It also has the power to cause spiritual death, death breeding death. The dead woman of "Ah, Are You Digging on My Grave?" is imaged as still having a kind of afterlife, at least in the ability to hear and speak. But the values which line up with a spiritual afterlife, love and memory, have disappeared. Those values are transactional, requiring a lover and a rememberer, and such are no longer present. In this sense the woman's afterlife has ended and values of the realistic vision are dominant. Nor are those values totally castigated: as Auden tells us in "Musee des Beaux Arts," we *must* carry on with our doggy life. At the same time, the values of the romantic vision assert themselves when one adds, again in Auden's terms, that we should (but do not) pay attention to the carcasses falling out of the sky around us. The will to preserve love by memory in "She, to Him III" is likewise problematical, neither to be castigated nor praised. Just as the rejection of love's pain in "Revulsion" is paid for with a great price, so here to continue to love is paid for with numbness. To be numb to the pain of being abandoned is the speaker's method, in the image of the vane, for remaining true to the one who "kissed ere canker came." The culmination of her brave assertion to be true is a one-sided, decayed, dead love, with the implication that she too is in a sense dead. In passionately asserting her love, she is not numb or neutral, but she is certainly as drained of color and life as the male speaker of "Neutral Tones." It seems in the end not to matter whether one picks the response of the male to reject love ("He Abjures Love," "Revulsion") or the woman to preserve love ("She, to Him III")—the result is the same. Both are doomed to numbness and neutral tones.

A Sonnet Sequence

The four "She, to Him" sonnets taken in order form a sequence dramatizing the end of a relationship. The first two present the female persona's imaginative prefiguring of the end of love; she imagines love ending because of the fading of her beauty in I and because of her death in II. In addition, in II she becomes aware of a lessening of love. In the third and fourth sonnets she confronts the actual ending of love, in III hearing the "last Goodbye" and in IV examining her supplanter. As the end of love moves from an imagined possibility to more and more of a reality, the speaker ever more resolutely asserts her love. It is as if she is incapable of any other response. Woman is as single-minded in embracing love as man is in rejecting love.

Hardy introduced the four "She, to Him" sonnets with a drawing illustrating the ending of the fourth sonnet: "Will you not grant to old affection's claim/The hand of friendship down Life's sunless hill?" A couple is shown walking down the shadowed side of a hill. J. O. Bailey, in something of an empirical and literalist mode, identifies the hillside as the eastern slope of Black Down, thus making for a sunset rather than a sunrise in the drawing. The sunset suggests metaphorically the endings forecast by the speaker of the poem. The bright rays on the hilltop suggest the still-bright, intense love of the woman despite the setting of love, or the darkening of her world when love ends.

In "She, to Him II" it is the female persona's imagined death which ends a love which is already in "decline." She further imagines her lover remembering her with a "thin thought, in two small words conveyed"—"Poor jade!" This leads her to examine thought; she concludes, painfully and angrily, that just as she will exist for him after death only as an infrequent thought (small letter "t"), so now in life she also exists for him only as that same thin thought while he is her whole life's Thought (capital "T"). This sonnet makes love woman's whole aim, the only Thought she is capable of, while man is capable of many thoughts and thus more truly a thinking being. Woman is identified with feeling, man with intellect, in an unsurprising conformity with Western tradition dating at least to the early church's understanding of the Adam and Eve story.

In "She, to Him IV," as in "She, to Him III," it is the beloved's faithlessness that ends love. Though the speaker curses the one who has supplanted her ("I can but maledict her, pray her dead,/For giving love and getting love of thee"), she continues to assert her love in a vision of marital communion:

> How much I love I know not, life not known,
> Save as one unit I would add love by;
> But this I know, my being is but thine own—
> Fused from its separateness by ecstasy.

Given that so far in the poetry we have seen no fusion of the dualities into a single, satisfying vision, the fusion of two other opposites, male and female in marriage, would seem equally problematical. At least this is the dualistic vision of Hardy's male personae. The female speaker here does not see it that way. While not specifically a part of the love story told in these four sonnets, the other early poems in the female persona could be fitted to this story sequence. "Her Confession" would come before the "She, to Him" sonnets, for its speaker does not as openly admit her love as the later speakers do. "Her Reproach" would come near "She, to Him II," for in both poems the speaker is just beginning to realize an impediment to her love. A slightly later poem, from 1873, "She at His Funeral," would finish the sequence, because the beloved undergoes actual rather than imagined death.

"Her Confession" describes an early moment in the blossoming of love, when there is still a defensiveness fighting with the desire to proclaim openly one's intensity of feeling:

> As some bland soul, to whom a debtor says
> "I'll now repay the amount I own to you,"
> In inward gladness feigns forgetfulness
> That such a payment ever was his due
>
> (His long thought notwithstanding), so did I
> At our last meeting waive your proffered kiss
> With quick divergent talk of scenery nigh,
> With such suspension to enhance my bliss.
>
> And as his looks in consternation fall
> When, gathering that the debt is lightly deemed,
> The debtor makes as not to pay at all,
> So faltered I, when your intention seemed
>
> Converted by my false uneagerness
> To putting off forever the caress.

There are two reasons for the woman's feigned indifference. The first is to enhance her bliss. This reason recalls the sentiments of "The Minute Before Meeting," which makes quite explicit that time is an enemy who will steal bliss. It is not only "moment after moment" that we die ("A Young Man's Exhortation"), but also moment by moment that "what is now about to be/Will all have been" ("The Minute Before Meeting"). The knowledge of time's hurtful power causes the speaker to suspend pleasure. She holds it in the future, free from the power of time to end it. But by so doing she of course also denies herself pleasure. In winning her victory she loses. Again Hardy is battling here with Time, an old enemy for him even in his twenties, and finding that win or lose one really loses.

The second reason for the woman's indifference is protection from a response by the male which would show him to care less intensely (about the debt or the love) than she cares (for she has been thinking long of the debt/love). The picture of love as an economic transaction admits an economic outcome of gain or loss. In the financial terms of the woman's metaphor, to lend love without receiving a repayment in kind results in loss. Thus in a poem concentrating on the early bloom of love, Hardy shows his female speaker confronting the possibility of pain and loss with more coyness and less openness than in the "She, to Him" poems. The female personae seem to become more direct and more impassioned in their assertions of constancy as the end of love becomes more certain.

"Her Reproach" takes us a stage further in the love story, to about the same time as "She, to Him II," when the woman realizes that something is beginning to lessen love. The speaker seems to be a woman in the position of Hardy's first wife Emma, feeling neglected by her man's pursuit of fame as a scholar or writer:

> Con the dead page as 'twere live love: press on!
> Cold wisdom's words will ease thy track for thee;
> Aye, go; cast off sweet ways, and leave me wan
> To biting blasts that are intent on me.
>
> But if thy object Fame's far summit be,
> Whose inclines many a skeleton overlies
> That missed both dream and substance, stop and see
> How absence wears these cheeks and dims these eyes!
>
> It surely is far sweeter and more wise
> To water love, than toil to leave anon
> A name whose glory-gleam will but advise
> Invidious minds to eclipse it with their own,
>
> And over which the kindliest will but stay
> A moment; musing, "He, too, had his day!"

The woman's reproach consists in reminding her beloved of the corollaries to his choice of earthly Fame. Fame is removed and distant, a far summit. The ascent to Fame is through "cold" wisdom. Fame is impermanent; its gleams will be eclipsed by others. Fame is on the side of darkness, for it leads to eclipse. Fame is on the side of death, the path to its summit littered with skeletons. Opposed to it are the values of love, which are the values of life, growth, sweetness. Aware of love's imperfection (the reason for her reproach), this poem's speaker nevertheless chooses to argue for the values love represents. The woman is again identified with feelings, the man with intellect.

"She at His Funeral" provides a strong ending to the preceding group of six early poems in the female voice. This group has moved from the growth of love to a lessening of its intensity to its imagined ending and to its actual ending when the beloved chooses a new lover. In this later poem love's end is even more permanent, with the physical death of the beloved:

> They bear him to his resting-place—
> In slow procession sweeping by;
> I follow at a stranger's space;
> His kindred they, his sweetheart I.
> Unchanged my gown of garish dye,
> Though sable-sad is their attire.
> But they stand round with griefless eye,
> Whilst my regret consumes like fire!

Just as ending is most permanent in this poem, through physical death, so loving is also most intense in this poem, consuming the speaker despite the hopelessness of any reciprocation. The irony which this poem turns on is an opposition between inner and outer. In outer form, the dead man's kin are closest to him, though their eyes are griefless. In outer form, the speaker has no official relationship to her beloved, and in her garish-colored dress appears indifferent to the grief and solemnity of the situation; she is an outsider, perhaps also in terms of class, excluded from the ceremony. Hardy's drawing makes this clear by placing her outside the wall of the churchyard. Though her gown proclaims her coldly unaffected by the death, inside the garish form, of course, she is consumed with fire. She stands in this poem identified with love, feeling, light, and warmth, and with affirmation in the face of death. Opposed to these qualities are formality, intellect, forgetfulness, and coldness. Death, unfortunately, belongs on both sides of the equation, with the dead man and his unfeeling kin on one side and on the other a woman who feels so deeply that it has consumed her. Again the empirical trap is sprung, as love is deconstructed into death.

Chapter 3
The Uses of the Female Voice

Hardy's early female-voiced poems, I hope I have shown, function differently from those with male speakers. What is the import of this for Hardy? For starters, these poems show men and women as another division in the world, *man/intellect* opposed to *woman/feeling*. This particular duality has a long religious and social tradition which has been held responsible for, among other things, the denial of education and opportunity to women and the entrapment of men in patriarchal roles which deny other human qualities.[2] If all Hardy is doing is reinforcing patriarchal stereotypes, then there is little point in reading the poems discussed in this chapter; Coventry Patmore's *Angel in the House* does a much fuller job of presenting the stereotypes. Hardy's female speakers are better looked at on a symbolic rather than a social level. In Hardy's empirically run universe, the qualities associated with *male* are also those associated with the forces governing the universe: cold, unfeeling, unaware, time-bound, mechanistic, dead, and above all true (as decided by intellect operating scientifically on observable physical phenomena). The qualities of the female are those of humankind living in the universe: warm, conscious, caring, able to feel pain, desirous of kindness and an end to suffering, and above all powerless to effect any change in the way things are. Just as on the domestic level in these poems the male is cruel to the female who nonetheless is constant in her love, so on the cosmic level the universe is cruel to humankind which nonetheless persists in desiring "some blessed Hope." Just as the woman seems to be incapable of any response other than to love, so humankind cannot help but to remain conscious of pain, unless it chooses to end awareness by an act of mass suicide. Woman, powerless on a social level, is a metaphor for humankind's equally powerless and alienated position in the universe. The single-mindedness of the women in these poems is a function of their emotional response to the world. The values allied with the female in Hardy's scheme—most especially desire—help her to override any recognition of what the world is in order to persevere in a quest for the ideal, with tremendous constancy in the face of every kind of death, decay, and destruction. The male, allied as he is with the truth of empiricism and yet also desirous of the beauty of the woman's vision, is more complex than the female. His vision is dual and he is not able to override his "reasonable" side, as is the female, to persevere as she does. She is more heroic, but also more stupid. Peter Casagrande highlights Hardy's swipe at women in *Desperate Remedies* (1871): "it is well to remember that the brighter endurance of women at these epochs—invaluable, sweet, angelic, as it is—owes some of its origin to a *narrower vision* that shuts out many of the leaden-eyed despairs in the van, than to a hopefulness intense enough to quell them" (*Unity in Hardy's Novels*, 76, italics mine). Woman's single-mindedness is not that far removed from the impercipient at a cathedral service, in the poem by that name, who smugly and foolishly remain a "bright believing band" who hear "the glorious distant sea" when to Hardy the sound is of a "dark and windswept pine." The otherness of the female makes the position of the male in the universe—that is, Hardy's personal position— even more alone, more alien. The single-mindedness of the female is thus used by Hardy to illustrate the division between male and female. Her ability to override the dualistic vision illustrates, paradoxically, the essential division and aloneness of humankind in the world. It also illustrates for Hardy the essential correctness of the dual vision of things.

Notes

1. Of the twenty early poems mentioned so far, seventeen have a male speaker; in the three with a female speaker, the topic is not love: "Dream of the City Shopwoman," "From Her in the Country," "The Ruined Maid." "Postponement" has for its persona a male bird who mourns the fickleness of females who nest in the evergreen tree (marry for money); as a type it belongs with the poems with a male speaker. The remaining early poem, "The Bride-Night Fire," unlike the other twenty-seven, is a long ballad rather than a lyric, in something of the dialect style of William Barnes. It was the first poem Hardy ever got published, solicited in 1875 by the editor of *Gentleman's Magazine*, who wanted "a short sketch, or brief story, or an article" (Bailey, *The Poetry of Thomas Hardy*, 106) from the up-and-coming novelist; Hardy took a chance on a poem.

2. Still the best primer on the religious tradition is E. M. W. Tillyard's *The Elizabethan World Picture* (New York: Macmillan, 1944). The social tradition in the Nineteenth Century is discussed by Wendell Stacy Johnson in *Sex and Marriage in Victorian Poetry* (Ithaca, N.Y.: Cornell University Press, 1975); John R. Reed in *Victorian Conventions* (Columbus: Ohio University Press, 1975); Lawrence Stone, *Road to Divorce: A History of the Making and Breaking of Marriage in England* (Oxford: Oxford University Press, 1990); and Michael Mason, *The Making of Victorian Sexuality* (Oxford: Oxford University Press, 1995). The *man-intellect/woman-feeling* opposition can also be seen in two poems Hardy echoed in his own poetry, *Paradise Lost* and *In Memoriam*. In *Paradise Lost*, Adam is reason, Eve emotion. Their fall in Book IX comes about when they separate in the Garden, Eve-emotion going off on her own, unsupported by Adam-reason to withstand the logic of the serpent. In *In Memoriam* XCVII, Hallam is the husband who "knows a thousand things" and Tennyson is the wife who "cannot understand" but affirms only "I love."

Hardy's illustration for "She at His Funeral" in *Wessex Poems*

Chapter 4

Hardy's Double Vision of Language

> "I call the folk to life again
> And build their houses up anew."
> —William Barnes, "The Depopulated Village"

When F. R. Leavis declared of Hardy in 1940 in the *Southern Review* that "any real claim he may have to a major status rests upon half-a-dozen poems," what he chiefly derided in the rest was their use of language.[1] For Leavis, Hardy "made a style out of stylelessness." Leavis's own style in the famous essay is clever, urbane, allusive, and superior. He uses it to make Hardy into a Polonius, a Pandarus, and a miscegynist:

> There is something extremely personal about the gauche unshrinking mismarriages—group mismarriages—of his diction, in which, with naif aplomb, he takes as they come the romantic-poetical, the prosaic-banal, the stilted literary, the colloquial, the archaistic, the erudite, the technical, the dialect word, the brand-new Hardy coinage.

From Leavis onward, the topic of Hardy and language has usually meant just such a description of Hardy's rugged effects, which are seen as a defect either to charge him with or defend him from. Norman Page notes that, long before Leavis, Hardy's style was a target of critics. Lytton Strachey complained of "ugly and cumbrous expressions," and T. S. Eliot delivered the backhanded compliment that "at times his style touches sublimity without ever having passed through the stage of being good" (Page, 151-52). For the defense, Philip Larkin argued that such oddnesses as Hardy's use of "lipping" for "kissing" are exactly right, once one gets used to the initial unusualness of the word. Hardy's own defense of his lexical, stanzaic, and metrical experiments, that they were cunning and purposeful Gothic irregularities, was accepted by Auden, who called Hardy his teacher in those realms, the best master any aspiring poet could have.

More recently, Dennis Taylor's *Hardy's Literary Language and Victorian Philology* (1993) has laid out other more encompassing areas for investigating Hardy's use of language. For those who wish to further study "this tremendous cupboard of Victorian intellectual life," in Taylor's phrase, his book along with Hans Aarsleff's *The Study of Language in England 1780-1860* are required reading. I will touch on a part of their work in order to explore how language, the system, rather than individual items of language, helped or impeded Hardy in his poetic effort.

Hardy's statements about his art, and about language in particular, are limited. The language he used daily with such skill and studied over the years so keenly, as his notebooks attest, did not seem to have become for him an important topic to address in any systematic way. His view of language will have to be pieced together from what explicit comments he did leave, and adduced from his practice and the intellectual climate of his times. This will necessitate leaving Hardy behind for a few pages to give an abbreviated history of language study in England up to his day. The purpose of this piecing together of Hardy's view of language is to make clear another of the filters through which his experience of the world reaches us.

Theories of Language Origin

In Hardy's day one of the great questions still surrounding the study of language was its origin. The question of language's origin achieved its importance because of other philosophical questions tied to it. Indeed, philology itself grew as a science because it nourished expectations that it would throw light on such problems as the nature of man and how one apprehends truth. There were in the mid-nineteenth century two competing views on the origin of language, both with long histories.[2] One view maintained that language was a divine gift, which partook of the mystery of its origin. That is, words themselves were a revelation of the divine and could "mean" beyond the conscious knowledge or intention of a speaker. One can see this tradition at work in Chaucerian irony, where a pilgrim convicts himself by saying more than he knows he has said, or in Milton, who argues that scriptural events, if allegories, are still the deliberate allegories of God Himself.[3] In this view, language as a divine creation was seen to mirror divinity and to make manifest on earth the realm of the heavenly. But more especially, language was the chosen instrument of God for a more particular revelation than Nature offered, and so was worthy of special study. The objects of study were, of course, the Scriptures, and they offered two especially important texts about language, both in *Genesis*: Adam's name-giving in chapter 2 and the Babylonian confusion in chapter 11. Hans Aarsleff summarizes what these two doctrines meant until the seventeenth century. Adam, says Aarsleff, as archetypal man, was also archetypal linguist. Since his naming of the animals occurred before the Fall, when he was in a state of nearly divine knowledge, his names reflected the harmony then in the world. Word bore a natural relationship to thing. That is, if Adam "had called a camel a camel, then this particular combination of sounds expressed and contained the camelness of camel, the essence of camel" ("Language and Victorian Ideology," 365). The Babylonian confusion did not threaten this view that Adam gave to things their "true" names; rather, by reaffirming that the world's languages were one perfect language, it allowed for the hope that through intensive study some of the perfect meaning of the original Adamic language might be recovered. Thus language study was an important adjunct to philosophy and science, for by learning the true names of things, one learned something about the things themselves. In this Adamic or sacramental view, language has a tremendous hidden power and potential to reveal truth. No poet holding this view of language could ever doubt the efficacy of language as an instrument of communication.

The counterview began to take hold in the seventeenth century, spurred on by the growth of the new science and given special impetus by Bacon, Hobbes, and Locke. Bacon's program, which asked for independent confirmation of matters of revelation by observation, eventually, and perhaps unintentionally, reversed the order of the old hierarchies. Man's place began to shift from ruling Nature in accordance with his God-revealed understanding to now looking to Nature for that same understanding of his place in it. This shift is evident as a concomitant of Bacon's program announced in *The Great Instauration* (1620):

> For man is but the servant and interpreter of nature: what he does and what he knows is only what he has observed of nature's order. . . . And all depends in keeping the eye steadily fixed upon the facts of nature and so receiving their images simply as they are. For God forbid that we should give out a dream of our own imagination for a pattern of the world.

This new way of looking at the world demanded a new language, since language's purpose had changed from source of revelation to means for communicating one's observations of nature.[4] Bacon noted that less and less were men content to "understand a mystery without a rigid definition" (*The Advancement of Learning*, book II). Hobbes, once secretary to Bacon, carried on this demand for careful definition, asking that "when we reason in words" we begin our "ratiocination from the definitions, or explications of the names" we are to use, "which is a method that hath been used only in geometry" (*Leviathan*, part I, chapter 5). Hobbes especially shunned metaphor, though Bacon had freely used it, because it did not transmit accurate information. He ascribed as a cause of absurd conclusions the use of metaphors, tropes, and other rhetorical figures, instead of words proper. The ideal became the mathematical precision which Sprat set forth in his *History of the Royal Society* (1667), a use of language which would enable men to deliver "so many Things almost in an equal number of Words." This desire for a language standing in perfect one-to-one correspondence with nature is what Swift satirizes in book III of *Gulliver's Travels*, when Gulliver learns of the Academy of Projectors whose sages have a "Scheme for entirely abolishing all Words whatsoever": they lug around on their backs huge piles of objects about which they wish to speak.

It was John Locke who buried the sacramental view of language by his immensely influential view of language's human origin and arbitrary qualities. Locke stated explictly that words "came to be made use of by men as the signs of their ideas . . . by a voluntary imposition, whereby such a word is made arbitrarily the mark of such an idea" (*An Essay Concerning Human Understanding*, book III, chapter 2). Thus was the privileged epistemological position of language done away with. Communication takes place not because of any inherent relationship between word and thing signified but only because a word elicits in the mind of the hearer the same idea that is in the mind of the speaker. Communication, then, depends upon shared knowledge and experience. Without such a sharing, language is insufficient, and the groundwork is laid for the essential isolation and alienation of people not only from God and Nature but from one another.

This empirical view of language was unquestionably the predominant one in the eighteenth and nineteenth centuries. Jeremy Bentham's comments about poetic language in particular, but language in general, could as well have been made by Hobbes or Locke: "between poetry and truth there is a natural opposition: false words, fictitious nature. The poet always stands in need of something false" (*The Rationale of Reward*, book III). Poetry gives pleasure, Bentham allows, but so does the game of push-pin, and at least "push-pin is always innocent," whereas our languages, "rich in terms of hatred and reproach, are poor and rugged for the purpose of science and reason." This is the decorative view of language: language is so loaded with judgments that while it may be well-suited for decorating the findings of judgment, making them more available to the weaker minds of common men, it is inadequate for gathering the facts which judgment needs. The poetic response to the attack on any imaginative quality carried in language was most eloquently given by Shelley: "reason is to the imagination," Shelley says, "as the body to the spirit, as the shadow to the substance" (*A Defense of Poetry*).[5] By this defense, carving out a special realm for itself separate from the material world, to which it was superior, poetry also essentially isolated itself from that same material world. Poetry, Shelley Platonically claims, is the reality; but to a society in which the material world is the real one, this can be understood only to mean that poetry is a different order of reality, a fanciful reality, and this realm it is allowed to have by default.

Thus the most socially telling attack on the empirical view of language came not from poetry but from contemporary Christianity's battle with natural science. In the decades before and after *The Origin of Species* (1859) was published, language was an important part of the debate over origins. Chambers' *Vestiges of the Natural History of Creation* (1844) brought language centrally into the debate by claiming that the groundwork laid in nature for man to speak "was as likely to produce sounds as an Eolian harp placed in a draught is to produce tones." That is, language arose solely out of physical readiness in man. William Whewell, master of Trinity College, Cambridge, gave the immediate response to Chambers, but it was the work of Richard Chenevix Trench which did most to revive the sacramental view of language. Trench, in his youth a student at Trinity College, later to be Dean of Westminster, began in 1845 a series of lectures on language that were published in 1851 as *On the Study of Words*. Words, according to Trench, quoting Wordsworth, are "living powers" (4). God has "pressed such a seal of truth upon language, that men are continuously uttering deeper things than they know, asserting mighty principles, it may be asserting them against themselves, in words that to them may seem nothing more than the current coin of society" (7). Trench expands Emerson's phrase that language is "fossil poetry" by claiming that it is also "fossil history" and "fossil morality," that indeed each word is "a concentrated poem": "Examine it, and it will be found to rest on some deep analogy of things natural and things spiritual" (6). As Taylor points out, Trench is a complex transitional figure: nominally the defender of the "new etymology," in which a word's earliest meaning was seen as simply one stage in its developing meaning, he was clearly fascinated with the old "etymological metaphysics" represented by the still-popular work of the eighteenth-century Adamacist John Horne Tooke. Trench mediated between the new and the old as modern religious liberals such as Teilhard de Chardin do between creationism and evolution: he allows for the evolution of language but insists on its nonarbitrary, Divine origin, dismissing the "urang-utang theory" in favor of *Genesis*. "God," he says, "did not begin the world with *names*, but *with the power of naming*" (14). Trench's influence was immense in Hardy's day. He was largely responsible for the plan of the Philological Society's *New English Dictionary*, forerunner of our *Oxford English Dictionary*.

How did Thomas Hardy respond to this battle over the nature of language? On which side of the debate did he place himself? A glance at the books he studied carefully in the 1860s gives one clue—with the "rationalist modes of thought" of "inductive science" and the "historical method" which he found in *Origin of Species*, *On Liberty*, and *Essays and Reviews* (Bjork, 104-06), along with the introduction to the atheism of Gibbon and Shelley that he read in Walter Bagehot's *Estimates of Some Englishmen and Scotchmen* (1858). The Hardy who was in London and losing his faith was surely affected more by Darwin than by Trench and the Cambridge Apostles. This Hardy, who became empiricist and agnostic, argues strongly for the Lockean view. However, the Hardy who was "churchy" and a poet must have felt tugged by Wordsworth's and Trench's claim that words are "living powers." The issue is complicated further by Hardy's admiration for his old friend, William Barnes.

William Barnes

Barnes is best known today as the dialect poet who influenced Patmore, Hopkins, and Hardy. In his own lifetime, however, Barnes's chief passion was philology. Despite learning some sixty languages and publishing almost ninety books and articles on his favorite subject, Barnes remained an outsider; the Philological Society never invited him into membership, despite inviting papers from him, and as the *Oxford English Dictionary* was being compiled, mostly under the guidance of Frederick James Furnivall from 1861 to 1878, Barnes was pointedly ignored—this despite W. W. Skeat's instruction that seldom-heard provincial dialect words be cited, an area in which Barnes was clearly an expert. Barnes was likely ignored because of the eccentricity of one of his theories. Where Trench argued that ordinary words, "the current coin of society," could be found upon examination to reveal deeper spiritual meanings, Barnes advanced a more secular and yet even more extreme Adamic doctrine; in 1862 he published a hobbyhorse of a book, *Tiw*, which listed fifty root forms that he claimed were the roots of all the Teutonic languages.

In *Tiw*, Barnes valued for their own sake the root forms he had discovered, precisely because they were the originals. This valuation of English's Teutonic roots led naturally to his lifework, a program for purifying English of all its Latin and Greek borrowings. In his later books, Barnes invented English words to replace all "foreign" ones: *grammar* itself, for example, became *speechcraft*, *verbs* became *timewords*, *transitive verbs* were *outreaching timewords*, *conjunctions* were *linkwords*, and *synonym* was renamed *word-sameness*. Of course, there were more awkward renamings than these: a *proper noun* was a *one-head thing-name* and a *present participle* an *on-going mark-timeword*, but these did not bother Barnes. His program to purify English was advanced partially out of a practical belief that "pure" English was simpler and clearer, and thus more easily understood, especially by the provincial folk whom he taught and preached to. This he illustrated with a table, partially reprinted here, arguing that English minds would understand the words in column two by knowing those in column one, but that to know the words in column four, they would first have to learn the ones in column three:

1	2	3	4
brother	brotherly	frater	fraternal
year	yearly	annus	annual
call	calling	voco	vocation
fore	forewarn	promones	premonition
five	fivefold	quinque	quintuple
happy	happiness	felix	felicity

But it is clear from the many Barnesian coinages which nobody would ever learn (*push-wainling* for *perambulator* was severely mocked during his lifetime) and from his comments on the "abjection" of English as a "mongrel language" that more than a utilitarian concern for uneducated peasant folk was at work. Even if the Saxon word is not clearer or the expression simpler, the pure root is better because it is the original and partakes of the natural "genius" of the language.

It was this side of Barnes, the love of the old and the original, which most appealed to Hardy. In an introduction to Barnes' poems, Hardy lamented the fate of the native words Barnes had tried so hard to preserve and revive:

> since his death, education in the west of England as elsewhere has gone on with its silent and inevitable effacements, reducing the speech of this country to uniformity, and obliterating every year many a fine old local word. The process is always the same: the word is ridiculed by the newly taught; it gets into disgrace; it is heard in holes and corners only; it dies; and, worst of all, it leaves no synonym (Orel, 76).

Hardy's metaphor in this passage is interestingly similar to one of Trench's: language itself has a life history; when it is ridiculed, it retreats to holes and corners, dies, and leaves no heir. Hardy frequently and most unempirically personifies language. In the few references to language in the preface to Barnes, he speaks of it (with verbal echoes to Sidney's *Defense of Poesy*) as "highest-soaring" and "fast-perishing." To give language a metaphoric life like this places Hardy at a great distance from the empirical camp, which eschews metaphor and prefers a word to mean one thing only. There is a second way in which this passage allies Hardy with Barnes and the more sacramental view of language. Hardy's lament that a word dies "leaving no synonym" shows his valuing of a word for itself, for its irreplaceable, unique genius. Finally, Hardy's statement on language here is of a piece with his views on loss and restoration everywhere. It is especially reminiscent of his view of the impossibility of architecturally restoring old churches, given in a paper he read to the Society for the Protection of Ancient Buildings in 1906, "Memories of Church Restoration." The "silent and inevitable effacements" education has visited upon language are similar to the church "restorations" which are really an "active destruction under saving names" (Orel, 203). Both education and restoration, seemingly well-intentioned, have actually served to destroy something precious and fragile.

The Restoration of Churches and Language

Hardy's argument against the possibility of church restoration is a natural result of his construction of the problem as an irreconcilable duality: "in respect of church conservation, the difficulty we encounter on the threshold, and one which besets us at every turn, is the fact that the building is beheld in two contradictory lights, and required for two incompatible purposes" (204). A church is a "chronicle in stone," a relic to be admired by the outsider, and also a "utilitarian machine" which must be kept going for the parish, "to discharge its original function": "the quaintly carved seat that a touch will damage has to be sat in, the frameless doors with the queer old locks and hinges have to keep out draughts, the bells whose shaking endangers the graceful steeple have to be rung" (205). Hardy suggests as an ideal, but impractical, solution that the old church "be enclosed in a crystal palace, covering it to the weathercock from rain and wind, and a new church be built alongside for services (assuming the parish to retain sufficient earnest-mindedness to desire them)." This can never be a real solution, however, for even despite the financial impracticality, two irreconcilable forces are at work, the "artist instinct" and the "care-taking instinct." The artist instinct cares for the form, realizing that "the essence and soul of an architectural monument does not lie in the particular blocks of stone or timber that compose it." The true architect, as artist, desires "to retain, recover, or recreate the idea which has become damaged." But for a nonartist, a person of "average impressionableness and culture," the essence and soul of a thing lies in its "human association."

Human association for Hardy always took precedence over any formal concern:

> —an object or mark raised or made by man on a scene is worth ten times any such formed by unconscious Nature. Hence clouds, mists, and mountains are unimportant beside the wear on the threshold, or the print of a hand. (*Early Life*, 153)

> —the beauty of association is entirely superior to the beauty of aspect, and a beloved relative's old battered tankard to the finest Greek vase. (*Early Life*, 158)

> —the method of Boldini . . . is of . . . infusing emotion into the baldest external objects either by the presence of a human figure among, or by mark of some human connection with them. (*Early Life*, 157-58)

> —there is no real interest or beauty in this mountain [a picture of the Wetterhorn], which appeals only to the childish taste for colour or size. The little houses at the foot are the real interest of the scene. (*Later Years*, 27)

> —suppose for argument's sake—nothing more—that you carry the stones [of Stonehenge] to America and re-erect them there. What happens? They lose all interest, because they would not form Stonehenge; and the same with the Stonehenge which was left. The relics being gone the associations of the place would be broken, all the sentiments

would have evaporated. ("Shall Stonehenge Go?" in Orel, 198)

—there is surely some conventional ecstasy, exaggeration,—shall I say humbug?—in what Ruskin writes about this [St. Mark's, Venice]. . . . One architectural defect nothing can get over—its squatness. . . . This being said, see what good things are left to say—of its art, of its history! That floor, of every colour and rich device, is worn into undulations by the infinite multitudes of feet that have trodden it, and what feet there have been among the rest! (*Early Life*, 253)

This last comment, made during Hardy's Italian trip in 1887, was followed by the lament that all of Venice's beauties were exposed to "the decaying rain . . . driving one to implore mentally that all these treasures may be put under a glass case!" This, like his suggestion to place churches under a crystal palace, is self-defeating; for protected in a glass case, how would a building ever continue to develop its human associations, its imprints of human use (we could not now ruminate on a Hardy walking St. Mark's), and how much more difficult for anyone it would be to notice those undulations in stone at any but the most exterior and easily seen portion of an edifice. Hardy of course never seriously proposed putting buildings under glass (it is said here only "mentally"), but his admiration for the past over the present, his notion of the present as a falling off, a deterioration, is clearly evident in his musing.

A person with both the artist and caretaker instincts (such as Hardy), who loved both form and human association, ultimately faces an impossible problem, because he is "pulled in two directions—in one by his wish to hand on or modify the abstract form, in the other by his reverence for the antiquity of its embodiment" (Orel, 216). One can never achieve both, finally, because of the deteriorative power of nature; the "wear and tear and the attacks of weather make interference unhappily impossible." If nature causes the form to wear out, and if the human use which imparts the all-important associative value to material also wears out that same material, then what is a builder to do? If one keeps the old materials, the form will have deteriorated from its original conception; if one restores the form, the human value in the material, the imprint of worshippers on stone and wood, is lost. Once things are subject to the power of time to change them, deterioration and loss are inevitable, and restoration impossible. This is of course the same sense of loss and of impossible choice that pervades the poems.

One more part of "Memories of Church Restoration" deserves attention. Hardy fills his paper with anecdotes to illustrate his principles. The most important is the first, quoted here in its entirety:

> In passing through a village less than five years ago the present writer paused a few minutes to look at the church, and on reaching the door heard quarreling within. The voices were discovered to be those of two men—brothers, I regret to state—who after an absence of many years had just returned to their native place to attend their father's funeral. The dispute was as to where the family pew had stood in their younger days. One swore that it was in the north aisle, adducing as proof his positive recollection of studying Sunday after Sunday the zigzag moulding of the arch before his eyes, which now visibly led from that aisle into the north transept. The other was equally positive that the pew had been in the nave. As the altercation grew sharper an explanation of the puzzle occurred to me, and I suggested that the old Norman arch we were looking at might have been the original chancel-arch, banished into the aisle to make room for the straddling new object in its place. Then one of the pair of natives remembered that a report of such a restoration had reached his ears afar, and the family peace was preserved, though not till the other had said, "Then I'm drowned if I'll ever come into the paltry church again, after having such a trick played upon me." (Orel, 206)

This anecdote illustrates the loss of human associations through questionable renovation. But more than human association is lost. An old memory is violated, a part of the shared past destroyed, by the movement of the original chancel-arch. Even worse, a present moment is also destroyed; when the two brothers quarrel, their shared fraternal relationship is violated (to Hardy's regret). The violation of the material world has a spiritual consequence. And the spiritual consequence runs even deeper than fraternal division, for one of the brothers declares his intention of never entering the church again, a division between God and man. Thus a violation of the past has present and future consequences, and material substance has an intimate connection with spiritual well-being. When one notes that for each of his general principles Hardy is careful to give several anecdotes such as this—human associations, as it were, added to the pure, abstract, generalized form—one can see yet again the spiritual power inherent in language for Hardy. First, language teaches spiritual things, and second, language, when it uses anecdotes of human association, employs a "spiritual" method for teaching. The way in which the story of the brothers communicates meaning is far removed from the geometry-like definitions Hobbes wanted language to employ.

When Hardy writes about two other arts, poetry and painting, the congeniality for him of the sacramental view of language again becomes apparent. Hardy defined poetry as "emotion put into measure" (*Later Years*, 78), a definition which removes his endeavor from the Lockean purpose of language, which is to communicate ideas. Further, Hardy continually advanced a claim for the artist as seer of things deeper than what the scientists could observe. Here are just a few examples:

> —the most devoted apostle of realism cannot escape . . . the exercise of Art. . . . Not until he becomes an automatic reproducer of all impressions whatsoever can he be called purely scientific. . . . [The artist selects] with an eye to being more truthful than truth. ("The Science of Fiction," Orel, 134)

> —art lies in making . . . defects the basis of a hitherto unperceived beauty. (*Early Life*, 151)

> —[the truly poetic is achieved] by seeing into the heart of a thing. (*Early Life*, 190)

> —the "simply natural" is interesting no longer. The much decried, mad, late-Turner rendering is now necessary to create my interest [1887]. The exact truth as to material fact ceases to be of importance in art—it is a student's style—the style of a period when the mind is serene and unawakened to the tragical mysteries of life, when it does not bring anything to the object that coalesces with and translates the qualities that are already there—half hidden, it may be—and the two united are depicted as the All. (*Early Life*, 242-43)

> —in life the seer should watch that pattern among general things which his idiosyncrasy moves him to observe, and describe that alone. This is, quite accurately, a going to Nature; yet the result is no mere photograph, but purely the product of the writer's mind. (*Early Life*, 198)

In summary, the artist perceives the unperceived, sees into the heart of things, does not merely photograph but translates half-hidden qualities, coalescing scientific observations with his deep-seeing to give a vision "more truthful than truth."[6]

One of Hardy's metaphors for this kind of insightful seeing is an updated version of the medieval notion of visible outer layer hiding precious inner substance, seen for example in the admonition at the end of the "Nun's Priest's Tale," "Taketh the fruit, and lat the chaf be stille." The tradition of grain and chaff, husk and kernel, is biblical. St. Augustine interpreted the text "the letter kills" (Hardy's epigraph for *Jude the Obscure*) "but the spirit gives life" to mean that "the letter covers the spirit as the chaff covers the grain. But to eat the chaff is to be a beast of burden; to eat the grain is to be human. He who uses human reason, therefore, will cast aside the chaff and hasten to eat the grain of the spirit" (Robertson, 58). In Augustine's reading one sees the close connection between language and spirit. Words are like chaff, but they contain a nourishing spiritual gift. Words are like a nut to be cracked to get at the kernel. Chaucer's story holds fruit to be extracted. Word and story have to be read in a way that will uncover the grain, break through the level of the chaff; since spiritual meaning is hidden in language, a spiritual way of reading is demanded, hence the famous four levels of interpretation in medieval exegesis. It is easy to see how poetry, interpreted for many centuries through this tradition, could continue to claim to teach higher (or deeper, depending upon one's spatial orientation) truths. And thus the agnostic Hardy finds himself again and again talking about issues of spirit, hidden meaning, and being "more truthful than truth," or using the shell-kernel figure: "Where is the Dorchester of my early recollection—I mean the human Dorchester—the kernel—of which the houses were but the shell?" (*Later Years*, 146). One cannot use this kind of figure without the weight of centuries of use taking over, so that the human Dorchester, as kernel, takes on associations of spiritual pithiness, and the houses, as shell, stand not literally empty but rather empty of meaning, an illusion of nourishment. Hardy's agnosticism should ally him with the empiricists rather than the sacramentalists, but his choice of the poetic vocation with its attendant tradition of speaking of itself in terms of "underlying," "hidden," "deeper," and "higher" truths leads Hardy naturally into a participation with a sacramental view of words. Indeed, his very Platonic statement on the power of names argues the same thing:

> A very good way of looking at things would be to regard everything as having an actual or false name, and an intrinsic or true name, to ascertain which all endeavour should be made. . . . The fact is that nearly all things are falsely, or rather inadequately, named. (*Early Life*, 284)

One way of looking at the job of the artist, then, is to see him finding out the real names of things. This is very close to the kind of etymological study that the sacramentalists employed, hoping that by going back to the original roots of words the essence of a thing, the "camelness of camel," could be discovered. The true name which the artist discovers is "no mere photograph" but "more truthful than truth," a point which Hardy made again in a speech at the age of seventy upon being presented the freedom of Dorchester:

> My Casterbridge . . . is not Dorchester, not even the Dorchester as it existed sixty years ago, but a dream-place that never was. . . . Nevertheless, when somebody said to me that "Casterbridge" is a sort of essence of the town as it used to be, "a place more Dorchester than Dorchester itself," I could not absolutely contradict him, though I could not quite perceive it. At any rate, it is not a photograph in words, that inartistic species of literary produce." (*Later Years*, 144)

Hardy's antipathy for the photograph and belief in the artist's ability to see beyond the facts into the essence of things put him at odds with the empiricists. For them, the camera became the invention that would put painters out of business. Some painters agreed. When Louis-Jacques Mande Daguerre publicly announced the daguerreotype process in 1839, Paul Delaroche is supposed to have said, "From this moment, painting is dead." But photography of course did not replace painting. Painting freed itself from representationalism and claimed for itself a higher truth, similar to Shelley's defense for poetry. Van Gogh said that his great ambition was not to create "a mathematically accurate head" but to achieve "inaccuracies, deviations, deformations and changes of reality that may well be lies, if one wishes, but are truer than literal truth" (*Encyclopedia of World Art*, XI, 318; XIV, 699). Van Gogh's ideas here are very close to Hardy's own conception of art: the emphasis on feeling rather than exact scientific or photographic reproduction, the valuing of the personal, if idiosyncratic, mode of regard, the purposeful introduction of incorrectnesses (like Hardy's own "cunning Gothic irregularities"), the claim to a truth higher than literal truth.

And yet the Hardy who so clearly seems in sympathy with the view that the artist is no mere camera recording facts but one who sees into the essence of things sometimes phrases his statements very oddly for one taking the artist's side: "however true this book may be in essence, in fact it is utterly untrue" (*Later Years*, 195). Final, emphatic place in this sentence is given to the untruth of art. When asked by William Archer about ghost stories, Hardy remarked that "the fact that I can't believe them to be true destroys them for me" (45). This is a curious reason for a poet to dislike an aesthetic object. It is like Darwin's account of Brazil during the voyage of the *Beagle*: "Brazilian scenery is nothing more nor less than a view in the *Arabian Nights*, with the advantage of reality"

(*The Voyages of Charles Darwin*, 40). For Hardy, too, fact held a special place. "Oh, but it really happened" was for him a valid defense of a poem (Hynes, 61). This idolatry of fact coexists with, perhaps occurs because of, an orthodoxy of doubt. Hardy knew with certainty how one is to doubt. In the poems, we have seen the certainty of impossible choice. "Memories of Church Restoration" gives the same guarantee that the artist instinct and the caretaker instinct cannot be reconciled. Moreover, refusing to choose is also not an option. The rain and wind wear down the church and one either repairs it or doesn't. The woman in "Her Dilemma" is forced to either say or not say a loving lie. So the world presents impossible choices and then further says, "Choose."

On which side would Hardy finally place himself, with the empiricists or sacramentalists? We can see portions of both views in his statements about language and might therefore posit that he sees the choice as a necessary yet impossible one. But Hardy does not lay out any statement on the language controversy. It was not a subject he consciously chose to shape an essay on, as he did on church restoration, nor is language itself the "real" subject of his poems, as with some modern writers. In this case, Hardy seems unaware of the problems caused by the competition between two views of language. This has resulted in some problematical poems, the subject of the next chapter. Untangling those poems will show something about the modernity and accessibility of Hardy's poetry.

Notes

1. F. R. Leavis, "Hardy the Poet," *Southern Review* (1940), 87-98; the six poems Leavis valued are "Neutral Tones," "A Broken Appointment," "The Self-Unseeing," "The Voice," "After a Journey," and "During Wind and Rain."

2. See Hans Aarsleff, *The Study of Language in England, 1780-1860* (Princeton: Princeton University Press, 1967), 1-11, and *From Locke to Saussure* (Minneapolis: University of Minnesota Press, 1982), 281ff. For a concise discussion of the two views prevalent in mid-nineteenth century England see Peter Allan Dale, "'Gracious Lies': The Meaning of Metaphor in *In Memoriam*," *Victorian Poetry* 18 (1980), 147-67. Gerald Bruns traces two language traditions in slightly different forms in *Modern Poetry and the Idea of Language* (New Haven: Yale University Press, 1974); for Bruns, the key difference is not language's origins but whether words are perceived as functional or substantial.

3. See Basil Willey, *The Seventeenth Century Background* (1953; reprint, New York: Anchor, 1935), 236 for a discussion of Milton's view on biblical language.

4. For a discussion of science and the growth of the plain style see Joan Bennett, "An Aspect of the Evolution of Seventeenth Century Prose," *Review of English Studies* 17 (1941), 281-97. Bruns, 35ff., traces classical and medieval antecedents for Bacon and Locke, de-emphasizing the newness of their view of language.

5. Even in Wordsworth's attempt to vitalize the mechanistic world which the eighteenth century had given him, one must also see the heritage of Locke, as in the lamentation on "the sad incompetence of human speech" (*The Prelude*, VI, 593) or the desire to speak in poetry a selection of the language "really spoken by men" (*Preface to the Second Edition of Lyrical Ballads*), bringing poetic language closer to the prose which the scientific tradition wanted, a more precise language purified of its rhetorical flourishes. Coleridge more directly disputed Locke, arguing that in poetry at least words are not arbitrary but take on symbolic value that unifies word and world: "how far is the word 'arbitrary' a misnomer? Are not words etc. parts and germinations of the Plant? And what is the law of their Growth?— In something of this order I would endeavour to destroy the old antithesis of Words and Things, elevating, as it were, words into Things, and living Things too" (from a letter to Godwin, quoted in Bruns, 43). A favorite metaphor for challenging the mechanism of the Utilitarians was this organic one of plants and growth. The oak tree especially is traceable through George Eliot, Carlyle, and Hardy as an image of the real nature of human life; see G. B. Tennyson, "Carlyle: Beginning with the Word," in *The Victorian Experience: The Prose Writers*, ed. Richard Levine (Athens: Ohio University Press, 1982), 1-21.

6. This is essentially Shelley's *Defense of Poetry*. For a discussion of Shelley's own use of language and his effect on Hardy, see Isobel Armstrong, *Language As Living Form in Nineteenth Century Poetry* (Totowa, N.J.: Barnes & Noble, 1982), 113-40; and Phyllis Bartlett, "Hardy's Shelley, *Keats-Shelley Journal* 4 (1955), 15-29.

Chapter 5

Hardy and Metaphor

> "Rather than words comes the thought of high windows:
> The sun-comprehending glass,
> And beyond it, the deep blue air, that shows
> Nothing, and is nowhere, and is endless."
> —Philip Larkin, "High Windows"

Allen Tate, in the same 1940 issue of the *Southern Review* as Leavis's essay, discussed a confusion in Hardy's use of language by challenging the appropriateness of the metaphor in the "philosophic" poems. Tate's example was "Nature's Questioning," a poem he found to be one of Hardy's "most powerful." The poem begins with the poet looking at "dawning, pool,/Field, flock, and lonely tree" and finding them gazing back at him, "like chastened children sitting silent in school." All the elements of Wordsworthian Nature are here to teach us we are not alone and abandoned in the universe, but those elements do not teach: they are schoolchildren, and they look to the poet to answer *their* questions. Tate argues that the tenor of the metaphor is so weakly perceived that the vehicle cancels out the natural objects altogether, so that it is the schoolchildren who ask the questions that are stanzas four through six. Both parts of the metaphor, children and nature, "suffer the neglect of the absentee God of Deism." Tate's complaint is that to paint this God as a schoolmaster, however severe, is a logical contradiction of this God's other qualities in the poem, where he is an Automaton, Vast Imbecility, or Plan. As such, Tate argues, this God "is not equipped to teach a class; he cannot even be present if he is 'impotent to tend.'" The metaphor argues with the metaphysics. Millions of students, however, in their pet names for their teachers, have agreed with Hardy more than with Tate.

To be fair to Tate, this problem is real and occurs also in "Hap," one of Hardy's first philosophic poems, and the best-known. "Crass

Casualty" and "dicing Time" conspire to strew pain about the speaker's pilgrimage through life when they could as easily have "strown/Blisses." But if the point of the poem is that there is no vengeful god, no "Powerfuller than I," then who are these other two Doomsters? By giving them metaphoric life, to obstruct and to cast and to strew, Hardy has undercut the metaphysics of the poem. Further, the word "pilgrimage" implies more spiritual purpose than the overt statement of the poem allows. Pilgrimage implies goal, and through long usage, spiritual goal. A pilgrim is a foreigner or wanderer; what place is really "home," then, for Hardy the pilgrim? Is there another home than earth? Not according to the rest of the poem, which here is refuted by the purposiveness inhering in some of Hardy's language. It hardly matters whether Hardy is or is not aware of this contradiction between language and metaphysics. In either case, we have an example of words asserting themselves in an almost sacramental way, creating meaning in a way that crosses the intention of their user. In this way, there ironically *is* a "Powerfuller than I" for Hardy to look to.

This particular controversy over the purposiveness of language in a world that doesn't believe in purpose is by no means a dead one. It is even more intense in our own century in which some of science's practitioners wish, as did Bacon, Hobbes, and Sprat before them, for a neutral, values-free, wholly unanthropomorphic language. As one modern historian of science says, "humanists may complain of the jargon of the specialties, sometimes with justice. But no science can flourish until it has its own language in which words denote things or conditions and not qualities, all loaded with vague residues of human experience" (Gillespie, 77). Such a language was also the wish of Jacques Monod, the French Nobel winner in molecular biology, who argued in his best-seller *Chance and Necessity* that objective scientific knowledge is the only kind of knowledge that one can rely on, that this knowledge teaches us that "living beings are chemical machines" (45), and that notions of purpose—beyond the "teleonomic" property of the living machine to survive in order to reproduce itself—are a lie. Just as Allen Tate looked to Hardy's personifications as a way to question his intent, so Theodore Roszak in a review of Monod's book also looked to the metaphoric basis of Monod's own language as a way to refute the scientist's conclusions, pointing out that Monod "consistently presents molecular and cellular activity as intentional, telling us how molecules and enzymes *choose, recognize, cooperate, direct,* etc. All biologists make sense of their work by way of just such a purposive vocabulary. Not even Monod can find another language to speak—because none exists" (16). Both Tate and Roszak are arguing in essence for a sacramental view of language, that there is a truth in how words shape our thoughts, and that by examining the metaphors we use we can most quickly get to that truth. This view that language, if not reflecting some divine truth, at the very least powerfully shapes our thoughts, giving us a model by which perception and cognition become possible, has achieved powerful status in our time. Note Gestalt psychology with its description of perception as a modeling or ordering or patterning of stimuli to make meaning; the Kuhnian view of science as a construal of reality through a model or paradigm rather than a depiction of reality; the Whorfian hypothesis that our language is the model which controls what we can perceive; Levi-Strauss's contention that the savage mind understands the world by imposing on the world analogical orderings. In this view, metaphor has become the key component of language.

Metaphor and syntax taken together show two ways in which the "vague residues of human experience" cling to language. The most obvious is syntax. The pattern of English syntax (subject-verb-object) suggests an actor taking action. This lends itself to anthropomorphizing and personification when the actor is not human. The result is such unintentionally teleological statements as Monod's, with molecular entities directing actions.[1] A way to lessen this purposiveness is the passive voice, which does not, however, do away with the subject-actor altogether but only hides "him." Another great indicator of human experience in our language is the metaphoric system of the language, which gives us models by which we construe our world. The taxonomy developed by George Lakoff and Mark Johnson in their influential book *Metaphors We Live By* (1980) claims the most for metaphor as an organizing force in cognition. Lakoff and Johnson argue that certain coherent, culturally determined groups of metaphors structure how one perceives the world. One of these groupings in English is *understanding is seeing, ideas are light sources, discourse is a light-medium*. As examples of these metaphors in use, they offer *I see what you're saying. It looks different from my point of view. What is your outlook on that? Now I've got the whole picture. That's an insightful idea. That was a brilliant remark. The argument is clear. It was a murky discussion. It's a transparent argument. The discussion was opaque* (48). In some theories of metaphoric language, these expressions would be considered "dead," no longer metaphoric—which Lakoff and Johnson argue is merely another measure of how powerful a "metaphor we live by" can be, passing from vivid comparison into literal truth. Colin Turbayne discusses much the same process happening in science when what is first proposed as an explanatory model is eventually mistaken for a literally true description of reality. As a model is repeated, Turbayne argues, it comes to be believed, and if it is sufficiently large in scope and if it gains sufficient credence, it becomes a worldview, or paradigm, as the metaphors of mechanism have become. Descartes and Newton, Turbayne argues, are examples of "unconscious victims of the metaphor of the great machine" (96), as is Locke, who attempts to understand the human mind in terms of a camera. At the beginning of a new millennium, the current metaphor for the mind as a computer has not, in this sense, advanced the discussion very far.

By once again making explicit what have become dead metaphors, Lakoff and Johnson give us another approach to Hardy. With metaphor, we have come full circle, back to the empirical ghosts of the opening chapter. Like those ghosts, metaphor is at the boundary line between the visible and the invisible. It tries to attach the elusive idea to the material world. To examine only one of Hardy's mechanistic metaphors, *the universe is a container*, could fill its own book. Within this metaphor one can see at work Hardy's deep concern with those two unobservable subjects, mind and God. The poem "Let Me Enjoy" from "A Set of Country Songs" would not seem, from its title, a fruitful place to look for these mechanistic metaphors. The poem is about Hardy hoping "to take advantage of the available pleasures of the present," as Frank Giordano reads it, but the poem quickly darkens and its last stanza creates a harshly mechanistic metaphor that undercuts the cheerfulness of the two titles:

> And some day hence, towards Paradise
> And all its blest—if such should be—
> I will lift glad, afar-off eyes,
> Though it contain no place for me.

The Lakoff-Johnson view of metaphor, since it claims that language at root is a metaphorical process (understanding and experiencing one thing in terms of another) makes for a larger "amount" of metaphor in Hardy's poetry than a more traditional view which sees metaphor as a case of special, not ordinary, language use. Where a traditional rhetorician would uncover no metaphors in the stanza above, Lakoff and Johnson can point to the word "Paradise" as an ontological metaphor, in which "Paradise" is an object "towards" which eyes can look. "Paradise" is also a structural metaphor in that it is imaged as a container, of places and people. Finally, the word is also an orientational metaphor in that it is "up" in this poem, as the eyes must "lift" to see it. The sestet of "Her Definition," looked at in chapter 2, also uses an image of Paradise:

> As common chests encasing wares of price
> Are borne with tenderness through halls of state,

> For what they cover, so the poor device
> Of homely wording I could tolerate,
> Knowing its unadornment held as freight
> The sweetest image outside Paradise.

The preposition "outside" gives boundaries to Paradise, making it an object divided into inside and outside; the preposition also structures Paradise as a box, an association strengthened by the poem's comparison of the poet's homely words to a chest encasing and covering wares. By implication, Paradise holds sweet images; one such image is at the moment outside its bounds.

The system formed by structural, ontological, and orientational metaphor here creates the impression that Paradise in these two poems is a real place, with boundaries that exclude and include. Is this really what Hardy imagined Paradise to be? What reality does this conventionally constructed Paradise hold for him? And what is its value if it is real? These questions are answered for Hardy by the culture's conventional metaphors, which paradoxically reduce a spiritual concept to a place (the mechanistic bias for locating all "real" things in space) yet also insist on elevating the value of the spiritual, placing it "up." The earlier discussion of "In Vision I Roamed," too, pointed out how the universe in that poem is imaged as a container, a "monstrous Dome" with "chambers" and "ghast heights of sky." The preposition "in" is also metaphorical in the lines "I lived unware, uncaring all that lay/Locked in that Universe taciturn and drear." In Hardy's implied metaphor *the universe is a container*, however, the universe is not inert. It has life: taciturn though it may be (that is, almost always silent), the universe yet has some slight ability to not be silent. This almost-personification of the universe is like Hardy's many personifications of God and Nature in the philosophical poems. In a poem like "Hap," the giving of human qualities to impersonal forces, which is next to impossible to avoid once one chooses to dramatize those forces, suggests that language is fighting Hardy. But these disconnects between language and metaphysics may also be seen as Hardy fighting the conventional associations of language, what Robert Bly in conversation once called the difficulty for a poet of using language that "has battlefields and armor and wagon wheels hanging off of it." Hardy's famously awkward personifications, such as "Lord Doom," "King Decay," "Mother Nature," and so on, are, in Tate's view, self-defeating attempts at describing a purposeless universe in unwittingly purposeful language. Another view might be that by personifying his forces, Hardy is actually undercutting what for him is a metaphor of purposiveness with centuries of positive accretions around it—God. Hardy may mean for us to *see through* "Time" and "Decay" as gods; they are purposely ridiculous figures, like the exploded (as Hardy would say, exploded for all thinking men) Christian God. By anthropomorphizing the forces in the universe, Hardy can both debunk the Christian God and still communicate his sense of the mysteriously almost-alive nature of the universe he lived in. A poem such as the "The Darkling Thrush," however, shows that an almost-alive universe can also be seen as an almost-dead one.

Problem Poems

For Tate, the philosophical poems with their personifications of the forces of nature are problem poems. I am suggesting that Hardy, a poet and not a philosopher, is doing what all poets attempt to do, work with language rather than be led by it. And yet, poems which violate the consistency of the culturally coherent system of metaphor do seem to argue, not surprisingly, that the issue of transcendence is a confusing one for Hardy, and certainly for Victorian society, whether it wishes to acknowledge it or not. As an example let me offer "Jubilate." Hardy presents "Jubilate" as a kind of ghost story told within a frame. A man that the poem's speaker "had met with somewhere before,/But how or when I now could recall no more" tells a story, somewhat in the manner of Coleridge's ancient mariner cornering the wedding guest. The teller and the auditor are in a pub, with the noises of celebration not far away. The story within the frame is set in a graveyard at one in the morning in winter, with the moonlight "spread out as a sea across the frozen snow," and the "yew-tree arms, glued hard to the stiff stark air." The pub-crawler relates that he was walking by the churchyard wall when he was halted at a "shut-in sound" of fiddles and tambourines. He looked, "as it were through a crystal roof," and saw "a great company/Of the dead minueting in stately step underground," singing in chorus "We are out of it all!—yea, in Little-Ease cramped no more!" The watcher by the graveyard wall takes this vision as a sign that he will soon join them. Hardy ends the poem melodramatically, with the man emptying the dregs of his cup and leaving the pub, where "the darkness swallowed him up."

The dancers' shout "We are out of it all!" indicates an ontological metaphor (*life is a container or room*). Death is rather commonly seen this way, as an exit or leave-taking. In the poem's last line "swallowed" is also an ontological metaphor (*darkness is a living being*) and "up" indicates an orientational metaphor. Darkness and the dancing company, both down in the poem, argue with the language's larger system of coherence for the orientational metaphors up and down: conscious is up ("wake up"), unconscious down ("he sank into a coma"); health and life are up ("peak of health," "top shape"), sickness and death down ("declining health," "he dropped dead"), and so on. Jubilation and dancing are not commonly ascribed to the dead, except perhaps in the religious imagination, and there the orientation would not be downward. The afterlife created in this poem dislocates the Christian afterlife and yet perserves some aspects of it. Further, it raises again the perplexing question of an afterlife's reality. What place is outside the world?

"Haunting Fingers" (subtitled "A Phantasy in a Museum of Musical Instruments") wrestles with the same problem. In this poem musical instruments are treated metaphorically as sentient beings. The contrabasso brags that it once could wake the populace "to passioned pulsings past their will." Set against the life of the instruments, the populace seem less alive, almost automatons, similar to the pulsing, twitching humans of *The Dynasts* who are moved past their will by the Immanent Will. The viol adds "Much tune have I set free/To spur the dance," and again humans are acted upon by the instruments. The shawm tells us that "hymn and psalm/Poured from devout souls." Souls, standing for people, are containers out of which are poured song. Song, too, is an object, to be poured or to be set free. "Set free" implies that the container of the song is a trap or a prison. Thus while the instruments are alive and speaking and spurring and setting free, the populace, the souls, are objects and containers and acted upon rather than actors. In the last stanza, when day crawls in, the fantasy ends.

> Thus they, till each past player
> Stroked thinner and more thin,
> And the morning sky grew grayer
> And day crawled in.

Presumably the instruments no longer have life and speech but are again objects. Are the souls of the poem then no longer objects but now endowed with some greater, more active life? Into what does day crawl? The museum can now be seen as a coffin, the place where the once-living are now dead. Where does the real life of the poem exist, in night or in day? Does daylight bring death? Is inner light for Hardy taking place in darkness? If freedom is getting "out" of life, where is this "out." The problematical implications of the "dead" metaphors of these poems are not easily resolved.

Hardy clearly perceived with Carlyle the need for new metaphors for old truths. He understood in Carlylean terms that the visible part of religion was clothes, of late in need of a new tailor; he hoped, for example, for a refurbishing of the *Book of Common Prayer* "removing those things that are shaken" ("Apology" to *Late Lyrics and Earlier*). But other ground-level beliefs are also metaphoric. Accepting these metaphors as truth traps one in their entailments, blinding one to what these metaphors hide. If one does not see *we are in the world* as metaphor, one is trapped through language by the entailments of that metaphor. This is how Hardy could say "I have always wanted to see a ghost." By not seeing his underlying metaphor *knowledge is seeing* as metaphoric, Hardy ultimately has to deny the reality and truth of his poetry, or at least the reality of those "unseen" ghosts in his poetry.

And Hardy, surprisingly, did severely question the value of writing poetry, saying in the last year of his life that he had accomplished all he had wanted to do, but wondered whether it was worth doing (a reversal from artists who value their calling very highly but doubt if the product ever meets the original conception). And yet that almost daily retreat into the study to write what is perhaps not worth the doing. In "Haunting Fingers" and all the many poems in which objects are personified, one usually finds at the same time a use of conventional metaphors which deny that objects, and even people, can have life. Thus the life that Hardy imprints upon the world finds no home, has no real resting place. And in a Newtonian universe, only place or location makes for reality.

"That is mere juggling with a metaphor," Hardy said once to William Archer, showing an empiricist's disdain for metaphor's truth-revealing capacity (46). That unexamined view helps explain how such metaphorical contradictions arise in Hardy's poetry. And yet the metaphors of mechanism and empiricism sometimes reveal a very beautiful, very unmechanistic dimension, evident in Hardy's handling of another version of the container metaphor: *the universe is a prison, life is a prison, the body is a prison*. This metaphor can be seen operating in some of the poems discussed in this chapter: the "locked" universe of "In Vision I Roamed," the "cramped" life the dead in "Jubilate" are happy to be "out of," the trapped song in "Haunting Fingers" which must be "set free." The metaphor of the body as container is frequent (the speaker of "She, to Him I," for example, asks us to recall "the excellencies I once enshrined"). Most often the body is an ill-fitting container which acts like a restraint. In "I Look into My Glass," the speaker looking into the mirror wishes his heart "had shrunk as thin" as his body (a container now grown smaller) but finds instead that his "fragile frame" still feels as intensely as when at its prime. Abstractions too are uncomfortably small containers. "Heaven's high human scheme" is "hemmed within the coasts" of earth's shadow on the moon in "At a Lunar Eclipse." People in "The Two Houses" find themselves "each in his misery, irk, or joy," the emotions a container holding the people. "Thought" is "the Whole Life wherein my part was played" in "She, to Him II," "thought" here a theater-like container which allows life too little scope. In "Going and Staying," the third stanza's image of Time with his ghostly arms revolving changes in the final two lines to an image of a vat containing sinister and sublime.

Hardy's view of life as a prison is explicitly shown in this comment on Londoners:

> The roar of London! What is it composed of? Hurry, speech, laughters, moans, cries of little children. The people in this tragedy laugh, sing, smoke, toss off wines, etc., make love to girls in drawing-rooms; and yet are playing their parts in the tragedy just the same. Some wear jewels and feathers, some wear rags. All are caged birds; the only difference lies in the size of the cage. (*Early Life*, 224)

As he later told William Archer, "the material world is so uninteresting, human life is so miserably bounded, circumscribed, cabin'd, cribb'd, confined. I want another domain for the imagination to expatiate in" (45). Note that even when Hardy images a way out of his confining prison, he sees a domain wherein one can expand a little, occupy more space: in short, his way out of the container is to imagine a larger container. But it is the image of the cage or trap, especially the caged bird, that is most frequent, and shows the confining nature of body, life, and universe. Such poems as "The Caged Goldfinch" or "The Caged Thrush Freed and Home Again" explicitly deal with Hardy's revulsion at the act of caging. This revulsion had a strong personal element. One of the few early memories Hardy reports is of his father killing a bird with the throw of a stone (Gittings, *Young Thomas Hardy*, 19). Apparently the scene made an indelible impression on the young Hardy, for suffering birds appear again and again in his poetry and in the novels. Samuel Hynes uses this suffering in his parody of an archetypal Hardy poem: "A heath: winter: the sky gray: freezing rain falling: foreground a leafless tree: beneath it a bird that has starved to death: a poet regards the bird" (116). One thinks also of the many images of hunted, captured, or caged birds in *Tess*, or the scene at the beginning of *Jude* in which the young boy's kindness in allowing birds to eat the freshly planted grain from the field results in him being treated to the cruelty which he should have shown the birds. The random cruelty of the father's act may even have been transferred by Hardy to the father himself, as the male in the poetry is so often associated with the unfeeling powers who rule humankind with an often accidental cruelty. In one of his last poems, "We Are Getting to the End," Hardy uses the caged bird to image people imprisoned in the world unknowingly, "even as larks in cages sing/Unthoughtful of deliverance from this curse/That holds them lifelong in a latticed hearse." Not only the larks' cages but the earth too is a "latticed hearse," a prison bearing us to our end. There is an identification between people and larks as unknowing victims that recalls "The Darkling Thrush," in which the earth is canopied and walled like a crypt; the thrush sings as if it knows of hope, but a more detached mind, the mind reading the imagery of the poem as it is filtered through the speaker's mind, sees no hole in the sky allowing the song any exit.

The Escape from Mechanism

Is there any escape from Hardy's prisons? Donald Davie's 1972 book argued against it. For Davie, it was not just Hardy's self-effacement and passivity, his "engineered" rhythms and technological images that were imprisoning, but, not surprisingly, his appropriate-for-post-war-England pessimism. This pessimism Davie located not just in the poems but in the poetics, quoting from the "Apology" to *Late Lyrics and Earlier* (the famous passage on "loving-kindness" which Hardy thought demonstrated his meliorism rather than pessimism). Davie comments that this passage "makes it forgivable to think of Hardy, even today, as a pessimist," for the "immediate mournful qualification" of the words "free will" in "clause after clause, phrase after phrase, mirror[s] quite comically how in Hardy's system there is indeed a margin for human choice but the slimmest margin imaginable" (7). Davie's thesis was addressed ten years later by John Lucas in "Hardy, Donald Davie, England and the English," in the first *Thomas Hardy Annual*, edited by Norman Page. Lucas made the telling point that if a poet, to be great, must be radical, challenging the roots of his society, then that poet would end most likely as an exile, as Lawrence was and Davie himself became (145).

Davie's "slimmest margin" for free will withers away to no margin if one looks at the two poems Hardy chose to stand always at the end of the *Complete Poems*. In the first, neighbors, "tickled mad by some demonic force," choose to "hack their pleasant plains in festering seams," proving that "Yes. We are getting to the end of dreams!" The finality of the two end stops in that last line argues against pain being kept to a minimum. In the final poem, "He Resolves to Say No More," the speaker intones, "O my soul, keep the rest unknown!/It is too like a sound of moan/When the charnel-eyed/Pale Horse has nighed." As Hardy said, again in the "Apology," "a forward conjecture scarcely permits the hope of a better time, unless men's tendencies should change." That "unless" is a way out of the prison-house of a foreordained future. But just how far Hardy thought the tendencies of men could change is suggested by the rest of the passage:

> Whether owing to the barbarizing of taste in the younger minds by the dark madness of the late war, the unabashed cultivation of selfishness in all classes, the plethoric growth of knowledge simultaneously with the stunting of wisdom, "a degrading thirst after outrageous stimulation" (to quote Wordsworth again), or from any other cause, we seem threatened with a new Dark Age.

Where the radical Lawrence begins his poetic life with "Look! We Have Come Through!" the supposedly modest Hardy ends his with "Yes. We are getting to the end of dreams!" The future from the vantage of 1928, "too like a sound of moan," becomes later in the century in a Ted Hughes poem open and continual warfare, on a scale ranging from the nuclear to the domestic:

> This had happened too often before
> And was going to happen too often in future
> Blasting the whole world to bits
> Was too like slamming a door
> Too like dropping in a chair
> Exhausted with rage
> Too like being blown to bits yourself
> Which happened too easily
> With too like no consequences.
> ("Crow's Account of the Battle")

The famous violence of Ted Hughes's poetry is not necessarily an American import; the violation of the dream of loving-kindness in Hardy's two late poems points the way.

Richard Benvenuto argued for a slightly more hopeful view in an often-cited 1979 article in *Victorian Poetry*, "The Small Free Space in Hardy's Poetry." For Benvenuto, when Hardy moves to a personalized vision, moments of freedom and moral action are possible. When Hardy takes a cosmic viewpoint, however, his universe "appears as a giant prison" because of the strict, oppressive, and mysterious laws governing it. One example is "The Last Chrysanthemum," in which Hardy remarks on a single chrysanthemum that has waited too long to bloom and then corrects himself by realizing the flower has no mind to choose to wait but is "one mask of many worn/By the Great Face behind." Of this

Benvenuto writes that "from the cosmic standpoint the conditions of all things are uniform and the same, and the things themselves, like the flower, exist as disguises for and creature-prisoners of a universe of law." Hardy's last visions are darker than that, however, for it is not just a "universe of law" that imprisons us but our own human failings which put each other's lives in bondage. "The Gap in the White" shows this amply. Though set in the eighteenth century, as the subtitle "(178-)" indicates, this is a modern subject, the failure of dental science. The Cinderella-figure of the poem wakes to find she has cracked a tooth in the night. This hardly seems a life-and-death matter, but it does finally result in a despair unto death—not because of the laws of the universe (though bad timing may be blamed a little) but because of people's insistence on a standard of toothy beauty, an insistence that loving-kindness does not soften. Loving-kindness would seem to be the quality that both represents and allows for moral action, impelling Benvenuto's small, free space. In what poems does it actually come into play? In "A Broken Appointment" the speaker specifically calls for it, but finds it "lacking in your make." His reproach to the woman for not being kind, even though she loves him not, could have been matched by his approval of the woman in "Her Dilemma," who lied to be kind. But in the latter poem Hardy rails at Nature for devising situations that made such kindnesses a dilemma—somehow the praise of the woman's small, free moral action left out. It seems to be a *hope* for loving-kindness, rather than any experience of it, which motivates its appearance in the poetry. Absent love, it is looked for but not offered. And in the context of love, it chillingly disappears with equal completeness, for love is the most ephemeral of emotions. The lover in "A Hurried Meeting" learns this, as he imagines hearing a night-bird say, "You should have taken warning:/Love is a terrible thing: sweet for a space,/And then all mourning, mourning!" David Daiches, quoted in the introduction, is hard to disprove. I do not know of a single "happy" Hardy poem whose pleasant vision could not be undercut by a clever reader. If the small, free space of moral action must eventually succumb to necessity or fate or law, however, the personal response that belongs to it does release a power of its own against the impersonal, mechanical universe. If this is the sense of the free space, then all of Hardy's poems are free, for through them he is free—to be conscious, to write, to shape a vision. Hardy does not "succumb" to necessity until nearly his eighty-eighth year, after all, and of course everyone, not just Hardy, must succumb in that way.

Tom Paulin faced the pessimism charge head-on two decades ago with several well-chosen examples from the poems, rather than argue extra-literarily as I have just now done. The most powerful, because not easily argued for, is "During Wind and Rain." In a 1999 issue of *Harper's*, Donald Hall, coincidentally, chose the poem as the most beautiful lyric in the English language. The refrains of the poem's four stanzas are decidedly grim, though beautifully so: "How the sick leaves reel down in throngs!" "See, the white storm-birds wing across!" "And the rotten rose is ript from the wall." "Down their carved names the raindrop ploughs." And yet the major images of the poem, domestic scenes of timeless happiness, survive, Paulin and Hall both argue, in spite of these refrains. They are "each victories over all the interloping hostilities that will sooner or later taint, not them but the family we see so perfectly assured of their happiness going on forever" (Paulin, 209). That is, the family is doomed, but their activity, "the *yes* they are saying to life," transcends death.

This is one way to find the positive in Hardy's double vision. Another is to watch Hardy open out the ending of a poem. While characteristically Hardy becomes preachy in his last lines to drive an irony home, or adds a last stanza to show the darker side to a lighter moment or mood, sometimes he reverses the process, as in "Proud Songsters":

>   The thrushes sing as the sun is going,
>   And the finches whistle in ones and pairs,
>   And as it gets dark loud nightingales
>   In bushes
>   Pipe, as they can when April wears,
>   As if all Time were theirs.
>
>   These are brand-new birds of twelve-month's growing,
>   Which a year ago, or less than twain,
>   No finches were, nor nightingales,
>   nor thrushes,
>   But only particles of grain,
>   And earth, and air, and rain.

The poem begins with Hardy's disenchantment with nature. Birds stupidly pipe, sing, and whistle as if there were no death, unaware also that for them just a year ago there was no life; they have no knowledge of beginnings and endings, and so can be loud as the sun is going, not knowing what "dark" and "going" imply to the speaker observing the scene. They are "brand-new" birds, freshly manufactured, out of particles, molecules. This seems about to become Hardy's most reductive view of creation and life yet, when the poem slowly begins to change.

The birds are created out of "only particles of grain." This should end matters, for a truly mechanistic view, but Hardy does not end the list of elements that make up birds here. There is more than just grain to them. And grain itself connotes more than inert particle; it suggests food and growth—not at all the Detroit-like production of a year's new models of finches, nightingales, and thrushes. This list of bird ingredients expands to "earth" (and with this second item in his list Hardy begins to refute his word "only" in the phrase birds are "only particles"). Birds are also constituted from earth. Pause. And air. Pause. And rain. With each new element added to the recipe, the process of cooking up birds becomes less certain, less fixed. Yes, birds are grain, but how are they earth? And one thinks of Mother Earth as the deep source that brings to life the grain. How are birds air? One thinks of breath as the sustainer of life, and of wind with its Romantic connotations of inspiring life, and of the birds' freewheeling flight through the air. How are they rain? And now one thinks no more of birds but of the soft falling from the air to the earth, of a living motion connecting those elements and generating life, an image of grace. Just when the list should be most closed with the final rhyme on "rain," the list becomes most open: the loudness of the birds' piping in the first stanza is contrasted with the soft, thoughtful, increasingly slower reflection of the last lines, slowed by commas, a reflection on the mysteriousness and wonderfulness of creating song and life from particles, and of the wonder of earth and air and rain. The prison is open. Out slips mystery, joy, song. This is the situation of the man in handcuffs in "At the Railway Station, Upway," who as a fiddle begins to twang suddenly breaks forth in song: "This life so free/Is the thing for me." The constable smiles at this, but not just at the irony of situation. One smiles at song. This is also like the famous thrush who flings his soul upon the growing gloom. Thrush and handcuffed man are both imprisoned. But one should not as a result of that simply call the song foolish. No song is foolish, Hardy sings over and over again a thousand times.

Hardy began *Late Lyrics and Earlier*, published in his eighty-second year, with the poem "Weathers." Like "Going and Staying," printed a few poems later, its first stanza is an evocation of life's gentler pleasures:

> This is the weather the cuckoo likes,
>   And so do I;
> When showers betumble the chestnut spikes,
>   And nestlings fly:
> And the little brown nightingale bills his best,
> And they sit outside at 'The Travellers' Rest',
> And maids come forth sprig-muslin drest,

And citizens dream of the south and west,
And so do I.

The second section, characteristically, examines the other side of weather, but the lines maintain their noticeably gentle tone with a flow of alliteration and images such as rivulets and raindrops which are hardly apocalyptic:

> This is the weather the shepherd shuns,
>   And so do I;
> When beeches drip in browns and duns,
>   And thresh, and ply;
> And hill-hid tides throb, throe on throe,
> And meadow rivulets overflow,
> And drops on gate-bars hang in a row,
> And rooks in families homeward go,
>   And so do I.

This ending mention of "families" is rare in Hardy, as is "home"; the thought of him at last finding warmth and conviviality in the bosom of a family is so heartbreaking that one can only wish that at least momentarily it were so. John Crowe Ransom calls this "a deceptive beginning for the volume; it is refuted a hundred times" (5). There are actually one hundred fifty lyrics in the volume, but Ransom presumably is not making an argument about the remaining fifty. Whether the dream is refuted a hundred times or one hundred fifty times, it is still the thing prized first and placed first.

Another tack for explaining our felt sense that, despite the imprisoning imagery, this poetry is not imprisoning, comes from Donald Davie, perhaps inadvertently, when he remarks that "Green Slates (Penpethy)" is an "indifferent poem" that stands behind a much better poem on Cornish slate by John Betjeman, "Sunday Afternoon Service in St. Enodoc's Church, Cornwall" (111). Looked at not as a mark of Hardy's inadequacy but rather as evidence of his ability, muse like, to free another poet, Davie's comment opens out Hardy's poetry by opening out his influence. This "indifferent poem," to my mind, also stands behind one of the most admired lyrics of postwar British poetry, Philip Larkin's "High Windows," in its interruption of a speaker's musings to suddenly gasp in epiphanic recognition at "Green slates—seen high on roofs." Hardy has imprinted himself in the consciousness of our contemporary poets. The vague religious questing in Larkin's poem is a direct descendant of Hardy—the sense of loss of religious and moral values in its opening stanzas, the long slide, the desire to still look—up—

to high windows, and to the air beyond, the glass comprehending the sun while the poet comprehends, well, can only see, and what he sees is endless deep blue air. Larkin's poem could be called pessimistic in its vision of people going down a long slide, they think to happiness, and in its agnosticism about moral purpose (the windows, after all, may be only those of Larkin's flat in Pearson Park as easily as they may be those of a Gothic cathedral). But the poet still looks up. Seamus Heaney once wrote that although Larkin left Yeats for Hardy, Larkin could not "banish the Yeatsian need for a flow of sweetness" (132). Whether the sweetness is in the poetic line or an attitude toward the world, its presence as the other pole in Hardy's universe is witnessed by practically every poem. The awareness of desire, light, and hope is always there and has been there all along.

Note

1. Teleological language has been troubling enough to spawn its own subfield in the philosophy of science, with Ernst Mayr and Richard Dawkins most recently and notably attempting to sort out the problems with its use. Mayr in *Toward a New Philosophy of Biology* (1988), surprised at "how many philosophers, physical scientists, and occasionally even biologists still flirt with the concept of a teleological determination of evolution" (42), proposes a distinction between the purposive processes of individual organisms (to hunt, eat, grow, reproduce) and the non-goal-directed nature of species evolution. Dawkins, in such books as *The Selfish Gene* (1976) and *The Blind Watchmaker* (1986), similarly argues that of course the individual organism or "program" on the genetic level "acts." In *Unweaving the Rainbow* (1998) he examines how "bad poetry" teaches bad science, implying that there is a "good poetry," presumably such metaphors as his chapter title "The Selfish Cooperator."

Chapter 6

The Question of Hardy's Development

> "Always carry a pencil and paper."
> —Thomas Hardy to Robert Graves

Throughout this work I have been using the rather loosely defined terms *realistic* or *empirical* and *romantic* or *transcendental* to designate the poles of Hardy's vision. These terms have a different meaning in literary history, applying to certain historical periods and the kind of writing those periods or movements produced. It is in this literary historical sense that Hardy criticism has often tried to place Hardy, and the labels have been diverse: Hardy, it has been argued, is a Realist, a Romantic, an anti-Romantic, a post-Romantic, an anti-Realist, a Symbolist, an Impressionist, a Symbolic-Realist, a Naturalist, an Imagist, and of course a Victorian, Edwardian, and Modern.[1] This overlong list of labels would in one respect have delighted Hardy. Afraid of being pigeonholed, first as a rustic novelist and then as a pessimist, he vigorously defended himself in public and in private. He kept scrapbooks of critical reviews, now in the Dorset County Museum, with vitriolic rejoinders written in the margins. His characteristic answer to charges of a fantastic fatalism and unlikely coincidences was that "it really happened." He defended his poetry by always insisting that he wrote in personas, that his characters and their situations were creations, evocations of many moods, not mouthpieces of the author. His work could best be characterized, he felt, by its variety. We have it on the word of Robert Graves that Hardy's private response to one critic's all-too-familiar charge of excess pessimism in the poetry was to go through his latest collection with a pencil marking S, N, or C, according to whether the poems were sad, neutral, or cheerful; after adding them all up, Hardy found them in "pretty well equal proportions."[2] To Hardy, this proved that he worked in a wide range of tones. For him to be labeled by critics as both a Romantic and a Realist, both a Naturalist and a Symbolist, is to give the labels the slip once again by this same strategy. If he is all things, he can hardly be hanged for being any single thing.

Despite their lack of agreement on how to label Hardy, critics have almost universally rejected Hardy's claim that he wrote in a great variety of tones and attitudes in his poetry.[3] The critical response from the beginning has been to note a predominantly mournful outlook, at best neutral-tinted. When a poem speaks of the "mournful many-sidedness" of things, we nod assent to the first word rather than the second ("The Sick Battle-God"). So it has been that one of the enduring critical commonplaces is that Hardy, especially in the poetry, shows very little development.[4] Poems written in the 1860s stand beside those from the 1920s, and one would be hard-pressed to assign them to their proper decades if Hardy had not dated them. Alongside this truism stands another, that Hardy's poetry is a poetry of perception, based on careful observation of the world around. Much scholarship in the past twenty years has been devoted to modifying this view of Hardy as the naive or natural observer, noting that his eye was often ruminating on books as much as on life or nature.[5] Hardy was keenly aware of his lack of education, so that upon his arrival in London at the age of twenty-one he initiated a program of learning that could have served as a model for *Howard's End*'s lecture-attending Leonard Bast or his own *Jude the Obscure*'s Greek-grammar-toting stonemason. Hardy the autodidact often shows off his hard-won learning. He is a highly allusive writer, referring in the novels and poetry not only to the folk songs and legends of Dorset life, but also to the high canon of English literature: the King James Bible, Spenser, Shakespeare, Milton, Dryden, Gray, Burns, Scott, Wordsworth, Byron, Shelley, Keats, Tennyson, Arnold, Browning, and Swinburne. He made a study of painters in London's National Gallery, which he incorporated into the early novels, and he was fond of sprinkling Greek quotations throughout his work, especially from Sophocles, Aeschylus, and the New Testament. He took great pleasure in correcting the erudite Ezra Pound's Latin, objecting to Pound's title "Homage to Sextus Propertius" in favor of "Propertius Soliloquizes."[6] This bookish Thomas Hardy is the one Harold Bloom uses in *The Anxiety of Influence* to illustrate his notion of new writers wrestling with the strong writers of the past. Hardy, Bloom argues, steeped in Shelley, must overthrow him at every turn or else be himself conquered and silenced.

This literate Thomas Hardy has now entered our conception of him alongside that of the Dorset boy alive to the sights and sounds of a quickly vanishing rural England. But the other truism, that Hardy shows little development as a writer, seems unbudging. And yet, the modification of the first commonplace demands the modification of the second, for they are linked. If Hardy is a careful student of literature, and literature undergoes significant changes in his lifetime, then it would seem that Hardy would have noticed, and maybe even been affected by what he heard and read. Hardy lived from 1840 until 1928. The changes encompassed by those years were enormous. In 1840 Dorset did not yet have a railroad; in the 1920s Hardy enjoyed being chauffeured by Hermann Lea in a motor car (though he allowed Lea to drive only at the speed of a walker's pace, so that he could see the roadside scenery from that more familiar perspective). As a boy, Hardy talked with proud veterans of the Napoleonic Wars about their musket wounds; as an old man, he was sought out by damaged veterans of the First World War, Siegfried Sassoon, Robert Graves, and T. E. Lawrence, who would not talk of their experiences. In the early 1860s Hardy listened to lectures on the recently published book by Charles Darwin, *Origin of Species*; in the late 1920s he was reading Einstein, whom he included in the poem "Drinking Song." Along with these kinds of changes were many important movements in the arts: the Impressionism of Monet, born the same year as Hardy; the post-Impressionism of Cezanne, who like Hardy was revered late in life by the younger generation; Symbolism, brought across the Channel by Arthur Symons; Futurism from Italy; Imagism from Ezra Pound; Unanism and Vorticism and eventually, after the Great War, Modernism. Hardy, in his conversation with Robert Graves, claimed to be unaffected by all these movements, telling the younger poet that all they could really do was to "write on the old themes in the old styles" (307). But Hardy's own career looks suspiciously aware of the many changes in style over the nearly seventy years of his writing life.

One of the difficulties in tracing Hardy's development, as noted in chapter 2, is dating Hardy's poetry. The Hardy who ghostwrote a biography of himself, to be successfully passed off to the world for many years as the work of his second wife, was fully capable of disguising dates of composition or even creating misleading evidence. Peter Casagrande has suggested that the poem at the front of the *Complete Poems*, "Domicilium," which Hardy claimed as his "earliest known production in verse," is probably a much later fabrication, at least in part, to make him look like a boy-genius, a young Wordsworthian original. Brian Green has argued even more forcefully that "Domicilium" evidences the mature Hardy, that "far from being consciously-imitative neo-Wordsworthian," it is "deliberately modified para-Wordsworthian" and as such "instinct with the mature Hardy's usual ambivalence toward the plain words, portentous cadences, sinewy intellections, and moments of intense visionary joy Wordsworth is given to."[7] He dates its finishing or refashioning to 1916.

In fact, other early unpublished work exists, and it is not in the slightest like the long, fluid lines of "Domicilium" or Wordsworth. In the Dorset County Museum is a cheap, pocket-sized edition of Milton's poetry, the kind which workingmen such as Jude or Hardy himself as an architect's apprentice carried to read during any lull in the workday. The Milton is dated in Hardy's early hand "1866 Westbourne Park Villas." On the flyleaves one can see what must be among Hardy's earliest attempts at verse, two fragments, one a revision of the other. The more finished version is titled "Epitaph by Labourers":

> —All day he cursed and called us brutes:
> Then Time said 'James 'tis night!'
> Fear floored him: Shame pulled off his boots
> And Death put out his light.[8]

In the two pencilled drafts one can watch the young Hardy at work, borrowing a phrase from Milton to install in his own poem, as an apprentice would freely borrow a technique from a master.

Similarly, in his biography of Hardy, Michael Millgate prints fragments of an early note for a ballad, which begins

> I sat me down in a foreign town,
> And looked across the way:
> At a window there was a lady fair
> fairer than the day.[9]

The fragments are from three pocket-book pages written in the 1860s but torn out many years later and inserted in a notebook headed, "Poetical Matter." At this later time Hardy has added alternative wordings in square brackets as he begins both to fill out and revise the original piece, which is never finished. Millgate suggests that this working method is what Hardy means when he says that a poem is "from an old draft."

In his variorum edition of the *Complete Poems*, James Gibson pointedly regrets that so few of the earliest drafts have survived. The earliest which Gibson locates is "Song," dated "June 22. 1868." This draft, like the "Epitaph by Labourers" and the ballad note, is both heavily revised and unfinished. In what is to be a seven-stanza ballad about a girl named Hetty, Hardy has completed four stanzas, two of which are heavily reworked. Two more stanzas are but fragments, and one of the planned stanzas has no words at all. This draft appears fifty-seven years later in *Human Shows* as "Retty's Phases." Gibson argues that this working method is what Hardy meant when he told Edmund Gosse that he often jotted down parts of stanzas and ideas for poems when they occurred to him and put them aside "till time should serve for finishing them—often not till years after" (xxi).

It was not such incomplete attempts as "Epitaph by Labourers," "I sat me down in a foreign town," or Hetty's/Retty's "Song" which Hardy chose to reveal as his earliest work. Instead, he gave us "Domicilium" and twenty-eight poems dated from the period in the 1860s at Westbourne Park Villas, London. The manuscripts of these poems, however, are fair copies, not the original drafts. Hardy carefully added the dates (and sometimes the place of composition) of this early work when it was published. One need not doubt that the poems were begun when Hardy says they were begun to question to what extent the early work resembles the fair copies and the published work. Thus such a famous anthology piece as "Neutral Tones," which first appeared in *Wessex Poems* (1898) with the date 1867, has not had that date challenged. The date is important because the perception that Hardy's poetry changed little over his lifetime is built on the assumption of a sixty-odd-year career, from the 1860s to the 1920s. But Hardy's published poetry, with four exceptions, actually covers less than half that span, the thirty-year period from *Wessex Poems* in 1898 to *Winter Words* in 1928. The exceptions are a humorous dialect poem in the manner of William Barnes, "The Fire at Tranter Sweatley's" (1875), which appears in *Wessex Poems* as "The Bride-Night Fire"; two of the fourteen stanzas of "The Sergeant's Song" (1880), included in *The Trumpet-Major*; "The Stranger's Song" (1883); and an occasional piece, "Lines" (1890), written to be spoken at the Lyceum Theatre "as epilogue to a performance on behalf of Mrs. Jeune's Holiday Fund for City Children" (Purdy, 104). If one questions the dating of the early poems (those from the 1860s), arguing that they are actually revisions done in the last thirty or so years of Hardy's life, then the evidence we have of Hardy's skill at poetry before 1898 is quite sketchy indeed—a dialect poem from the early novel-writing period, a very short Napoleonic ballad, two pieces connected to the theater, and manuscript sources such as the fragments in his pocket Milton and "Poetical Matter" notebook. This evidence does not suggest an early gift for poetry.

"Neutral Tones"

"Neutral Tones" is crucial because it has, if any poem has, found a secure place in the Hardy canon. It is praised as standing out from the many run-of-the-mill efforts of *Wessex Poems*. If "Neutral Tones" is truly from 1867, then Hardy was already an accomplished poet at that time, and a victim of the bone-headedness of editors who rejected all of his early submissions until that first lone solicited dialect piece in 1875. It also supports the notion that Hardy developed very little as a poet: He wrote as well in 1867 as in that wonderful volume from fifty years later, *Moments of Vision*. But if "Neutral Tones" is a revision of an early unsuccessful poem, one more like the efforts in the pocket Milton than the poem we have today, then the question of Hardy's development looks quite different. The period from "Neutral Tones" to, again, *Moments of Vision* is shrunk to nineteen years, and the changes in even those two decades become more apparent. What I offer is not hard evidence, for none has been found (nor is likely to be, after the Max Gate bonfires) to prove the issue one way or the other, but a reading of the Hardy canon that asks whether he seems to be noticing the changes on the artistic horizon during the last thirty years of his life. Those thirty years can be characterized in the arts as a succession of movements, some originating inside little England but others coming from France, Italy, and America. The succession in one telling runs roughly from Symbolism to Imagism to Modernism. Hardy is usually excluded from this story of literary progress, in part because he is needed as an anchor for a native tradition that avoids all the French "-isms" in favor of a relatively unchanging Englishness. In this narrative he is the true successor to Gray, Wordsworth, and Tennyson; a bulwark against the un-English Yeats, Eliot, and Pound; father to the Georgians, Graves, Sassoon, and Owen; and godfather to The Movement, reaching its apotheosis in Larkin. If Hardy is to be the mentor of the Georgians, giving them a link to the Victorian past, he cannot be open to French influence, not Symons, not Pound, not Hulme, not Eliot. To develop along those lines puts the English tradition in danger.

When Hardy published his first volume, the situation of poetry in England was uncertain. Tennyson, upon Wordsworth's death in 1850, had admirably filled the role of poet laureate, bringing great prestige to the position and earning himself a baronetcy in the process. When Tennyson died in 1892, no one was immediately appointed laureate to take his place. No one could. After four years the government appointed a Conservative journalist, Alfred Austin, as a safe choice, a placeholder laureate, but Austin became more of a laughingstock with each verse published; the Prince of Wales, soon to be King Edward VII, was especially mortified by his laureate. The most popular poet in England in the 1890s was from outside little England, the young literary phenomenon from India, Rudyard Kipling. In 1892 his *Barrack Room Ballads* introduced a Cockney soldier, Tommy Atkins, who summed up all that was good and true about being English. Among the avant-garde, however, it was Arthur Symons who was the more respected. Symons's *The Symbolist Movement in Literature* (1899) famously fueled the development of Yeats in *Wind among the Reeds* (1899), but Symons's poetry, published earlier in the decade, had already brought the ideas of the French *symbolistes* across the Channel. The debt to Kipling in Hardy's first book, in the narrative poems about soldiers, is obvious, but what he learned from Symons less so.

Born the same year as Yeats and Kipling, Symons reportedly did not learn to read until he was nine, but was eventually fluent in English, French, and Italian. It was the French poets whom he especially championed—Baudelaire, Mallarme, Verlaine, and Rimbaud. His own poems, in imitation of these masters, often had the effect of Impressionist painting. Symons wrote poems in series, revisiting a scene to study its changing moods. One such series, titled, "Colour Studies at Dieppe," from *London Nights* (1895), includes poems subtitled "Rain on the Down," "After Sunset," "On the Beach," and "Gray and Green." This last poem carries the same title as a painting by the English Impressionist Walter Richard Sickert (1860-1942), who lived in Dieppe from 1885-1905. Sickert, who studied first with James McNeill Whistler and then Edgar Degas, performed the same service for English painting that Symons did for English literature, as the main conduit of the ideas of the French avant-garde. Symons translated Sickert's subtleties of scene and color into a poem, creating an effect of sharply delineated listlessness:

> The grey-green stretch of sandy grass,
> Indefinitely desolate;
> A sea of lead, a sky of slate:
> Already autumn in the air, alas!
>
> One stark monotony of stone,
> The long hotel, acutely white,
> Against the after-sunset light
> Withers grey-green, and takes the grass's tone.
>
> Listless and endless it outlies,
> And means, to you and me, no more

> Than any pebble on the shore,
> Or this indifferent moment as it dies.

I have found no evidence that Hardy read this poem, though it is likely. Hardy and Symons were friends, sharing poems and tastes. The Symonses visited the Hardys on several occasions, including a weekend with A. E. Housman at Max Gate in the summer of 1900. When Symons's poetry fell out of favor in the new century, Hardy wrote him commiseratingly that there was no longer anybody "to address, no public that knows" (Seymour-Smith, 677). The similarities to "Neutral Tones," then, are perhaps coincidental, but they are suggestive. The two poems share rhyme scheme and stanza structure, though Hardy's last line in each stanza is indented and given to trailing off:

> We stood by a pond that winter day,
> And the sun was white, as though chidden of God,
> And a few leaves lay on the starving sod;
> —They had fallen from an ash, and were gray.

The poems also share situation, theme, and mood. In each poem, the speaker and another with whom he shares an emotional bond are associated with a gray landscape, water, and diminishment. The theme of loss in both is treated lethargically, listlessly, as if great energy were lost with the waning of love or meaning. In an odd way, this listlessness or supposed indifference is the jaded nineties' version of the passionate exclamation of romantics everywhere that one will die without love. One doesn't die, these poems say, one just gets depressed and languid. A more psychologically attuned reading would argue that the poems' speakers are tired from expending so much energy denying the feelings of pain that come with loss.

Both poems' rhetorical strategies are also similar. The opening line of "Neutral Tones" establishes an action and a scene, which the rest of the stanza then fills out with almost total reliance on visual elements, primarily color and objects, to establish mood. The scene's limited palate of white and gray suggests both a stark instensity of feeling and a constriction in expression of that feeling. The painful limits of expression are suggested by the spare and minimalist nature of the scene: a few leaves, starvation, sod without vegetable growth or covering, an ash tree with its evocation of a burnt-out fire helped along by the nearness of "gray." Symons's poem, too, proceeds through a list of objects—grass, hotel, sky, sea, pebbles—and evokes its mood through a limited but emotionally evocative palette of white, slate, and grey-green. This, of course, is the Symbolists' program, subtly suggesting meaning through links between sound and sense and color. If anything, Hardy's poem is more explicitly Symbolist than Symons's. In its last stanza, "Neutral Tones" returns to its opening scene, but in this second time around those images have risen to the level of symbol: "Your face, and the God-curst sun, and a tree / And a pond edged with grayish leaves." Face, tree, pond, leaves, sun are now able themselves to create for the speaker (and reader) the emotions surrounding the ending of love.

When the century rolled over to 1900, there was a strong and almost immediate reaction against the decadent nineties. Suddenly fresh air in poetry was favored over smoky cafes, a vigorous realism over a dreamy languidness, and, for Yeats and Hardy, drama over poetry, Yeats with the Abbey Theater and Hardy with *The Dynasts*. The poetry which Hardy wrote in this decade, the first of the twentieth century, shows much continuity with *Wessex Poems*. But where that volume dwelt on his own and England's past, and something of a mythical past at that, his next volume was named, *Poems of the Past and Present* (1901), and the title was not a misnomer. For the first time Hardy published poems of recent experience: a section called, "War Poems" about the Boer War, then still raging; a section called, "Poems of Pilgrimage," a kind of travel diary of his pilgrimage to Italy to retrace the steps of Keats and Shelley; "The Darkling Thrush," to commemorate the coming of the new century; and only two poems dated from the 1860s, where *Wessex Poems* had seen sixteen. For the rest of the decade, Hardy continued to write lyrics, published as *Time's Laughingstocks* in 1909, but most of his energy was taken up with creating his great verse drama of the Napoleonic Wars, *The Dynasts*, for which he undertook research in the British Museum Reading Room, visited sites in the south and west of England, and interrogated living people as well as his own memory.

Georgianism, Imagism, Modernism

Satires of Circumstance, from 1914, was the next volume. Two occasional poems near the very beginning (they occur second and third) have entered the anthologies, and thus the Hardy canon, as certainly as "Neutral Tones." The poems are socially responsible commentary on public events, typifying Edwardian consciousness, if not opinion. "Channel Firing" is built upon an incident of gunnery practice by the British Navy in the Channel and is more prescient of the real nature of the coming war than anything else written for several years. "The Convergence of the Twain" examines the 1912 sinking of the Titanic. The year 1912 is now more remembered as the year in which Edward

Marsh brought out his first anthology of Georgian poetry and Ezra Pound invented Imagism. Georgianism is the movement that Hardy is more often associated with, especially through Edward Thomas, Robert Frost, and Robert Graves. For Hardy, however, the most important event from 1912 was the death of Emma, after a long and mostly unhappy marriage. This private event shocked the supposedly unchanging seventy-two-year-old poet into a series of elegies published in *Satires of Circumstance* as "The Poems of 1912-1913." Those poems reflect aspects of both Georgianism and Imagism. The first poem in the series, "The Going," mixes an older poetic diction with lines as pure, spare, and conversational as anything Robert Frost, Edward Thomas, or Ezra Pound could write: "Why did you give no hint that night?" "Why do you make me leave the house?" "Why, then . . . did we not speak?" Rather than receiving answers, the poet wakes each day to see "morning harden upon the wall." T. E. Hulme's prediction of a coming day of dry, hard verse arrived for Hardy on the day of this personal dry, hard event. Another canonical poem, from his next volume, *Moments of Vision* (1917), has often been singled out because it is strikingly different from other Hardy poems, though at the same time clearly in Hardy's voice. The poem is built on images which Hardy read in Emma's diaries after her death. It is an Imagist poem, though rhymed: "During Wind and Rain." Robert Langbaum (*Thomas Hardy in Our Time*, 39) goes even further, arguing for a predominating Imagist style in Hardy's penultimate volume, *Human Shows* (1925). We also know from Lennart Bjork's *The Literary Notebooks of Thomas Hardy* that he was carefully reading both Pound and Eliot in the 1920s.

It is not my intention, with these few examples, to argue that Hardy kept pace with each new fashion in literary circles, or that he could fairly be called a Symbolist, an Imagist, or a Modernist. It is important to note, however, that Hardy was not ignorant of the techniques of these movements, tried them out, and chose not to use them very often. He was satisfied with the old themes in the old forms, though this is a bit disingenuous, for he regularly invented new stanzaic forms for himself and wrote on some decidedly untraditional topics, such as modern dental science. That poem, "The Gap in the White," from his last volume, *Winter Words* (1928), is characteristic, I think, of Hardy's ability to adapt the new, when he chose to, to older themes and forms:

> Something had cracked in her mouth as she slept,
> Having danced with the Prince long, and sipped his gold tass;
> And she woke in alarm, and quick, breathlessly, leapt
>   Out of bed to the glass.

The Cinderella of this story will not have a marriage and a life lived happily ever after because of a small, very human accident: she has cracked a tooth in the night. The gap in her smile will be considered disfiguring by the society in which she lives. The poem ends by telling us, with Hardy's characteristically complicated perspective of both biting censure and unjudging detachment, that we will not understand her plight, thanks to modern dentistry:

> And if you could go and examine her grave
>   You'd find the gap there,
> But not understand, now that science can save,
>   Her unbounded despair.

Hardy probably would have labeled this poem humorous, rather than sad or neutral. But the humor, if we can find it, is of a rather classical kind, like that of Troilus looking down from the heavens on all the turmoil of his life on earth and uttering a laugh. For those still in life, the despair is real, the solution not so easily found, the disfigurements permanent and of lasting consequence. From this perspective, Hardy is able to indict society for the casualness with which it discards us. But from the detached perspective of Troilus, the speaker of "The Gap in the White" is also able to see that it is we who are the objects of mirth for our overblown human expectations to dance with the prince, basing our lifelong happiness on such a chance. From the first perspective, the poem is tragic; from the second, comic. This, I believe, better represents the "many-sidedness of things" Hardy claimed to be interested in showing, rather than a list dividing up the poems into sad, neutral, or cheerful. The note of mournfulness in the first perspective regularly drowns out for us the irony implicit in the second. Thus the double perspective in Hardy's poetry becomes invisible to us, submerged by this powerful note. We see and hear a sameness. One conclusion we draw is that Hardy, a one-note writer, underwent no development. But it is clear that he was aware of other ways of writing poetry, and quite capable of producing fine Symbolist and Imagist poems. His choice was to keep working the field that seemed true to him. Others, such as Ezra Pound, felt the need to "make it new." Others, such as Robert Frost and Edward Thomas, felt the need to purge Victorian rhetoric from poetry, to finish Wordsworth's program of more subtly capturing the music of human speech. Hardy recognized, it is clear from his frustrations with critics, that his poetry was often not getting through. His choice, however, was not to seek new ground or new tools, but to persist stubbornly in working the plot he was given. From this stubbornness and persistence we have nearly a thousand poems in thirty years, and a model that many poets have used for working their own gardens, to our profit.

Notes

1. Because his long writing life breaks into two careers, twenty-five years as a novelist and another thirty as a poet, Hardy has commonly been seen as "a great Victorian novelist who then became a great twentieth-century poet" (J. Hillis Miller, intro. *Jude the Obscure*, 1992); David Perkins in *A History of Modern Poetry* (1976) describes Hardy as "showing both 'Victorian' and 'modern' habits of sensibility and technique (145); the great Hardy scholar Samuel Hynes in *Edwardian Occasions* (1972) places Hardy as a central figure in that brief but important transitional period; Mrs. Oliphant's 1896 review of *Jude* associated Hardy with Zola and thus naturalism, motivating Hardy to reject Naturalism as true art; Robin Gilmour's *The Novel in the Victorian Age* (1986) explores Hardy's relationship with Naturalism; Frederick Karl's *A Reader's Guide to the Nineteenth Century British Novel* (1964) argued that Hardy was neither a romantic nor a naturalist but employed a "symbolic realism" (296); Penelope Vigar in *The Novels of Thomas Hardy: Illusion and Reality* (1974) called Hardy an "Impressionist"; but Ford Madox Ford in *The March of Literature* (1938) contrasted Hardy's technique to Conrad and Impressionism; early critics such as Harvey Curtis Webster, Desmond Hawkins, and Douglas Brown saw Hardy as a realist; but Albert J. Guerard's 1949 landmark study *Thomas Hardy: The Novels and Stories* argues for Hardy as an anti-realist; Robert Langbaum's *The Poetry of Experience* (1985) defines a late romanticism that applies to Hardy, while his *Thomas Hardy in Our Time* (1995) notes how Hardy "continues the romantic tradition of natural-supernaturalism" (30); Patricia O'Neill's "Thomas Hardy: Poetics of a Postromantic," *Victorian Poetry* 27:2 (Summer 1989), 129-45 cites his "objective realism"; Tom Paulin's *Thomas Hardy: The Poetry of Perception* (1975) sees Hardy as a "fence-sitter" between positivism and romanticism. It seems to be a tradition in Hardy criticism to offer a term to describe him which is then undercut as inadequate. My thanks to my colleague Rob Watson for his comments on the criticism of the novels.

2. Robert Graves, *Good-Bye to All That* (1929; reprint, New York: Anchor, 1985), 307. For Hardy's own defense of his work, see the prefaces to *Poems of the Past and Present* (1901), *Time's Laughingstocks* (1909), *Late Lyrics and Earlier* (1922), and *Winter Words in Various Moods and Metres* (1928).

3. Robert Langbaum, however, finds Hardy various, though he perceives little development in the poetry (*Thomas Hardy in Our Time*, 37).

4. Dennis Taylor, however, argues for development in the meditative lyric (*Hardy's Poetry, 1860-1928*) and divides the poetry into six stages of development ("The Chronology of Hardy's Poetry," *Victorian Poetry* (Spring 1999), 1-57.

5. Paul Zietlow's *Moments of Vision* (1974) was seminal in arguing for Hardy's powers of observation, including, however, epiphanies; Tom Paulin's fine book, *The Poetry of Perception* (1975), continued the metaphor, but also allowed, of course, that Hardy was imbued with other writers, especially Browning. One of the earliest influence studies was William Rutland's *Thomas Hardy: A Study of his Writings and their Background* (1938). Carl Weber's dated but still very sound study, *Hardy of Wessex*, lists many of the more overt borrowings in its appendices. What books remain of Hardy's dispersed library, in the Dorset County Museum, often contain annotations, especially volumes from the early years. See also Lennart Bjork, *The Literary Notebooks of Thomas Hardy* for a history of Hardy's reading. For further citations, see my "Once More to 'The Darkling Thrush,'" *CEA Critic* 48/49 (summer/fall 1986), 76-86.

6 J.J. Wilhelm, *Ezra Pound in London and Paris, 1908-1925* (University Park: The Pennsylvannia State University Press, 1990), 254. Rather than take offense, Pound took the letter, as Canto 80 has it: "leaving America I brought with me $80 / and England a letter of Thomas Hardy's."

7. See Brian Green, "The Composition and Publication of 'Domicilium,'" *Thomas Hardy Journal* (1993) 91-94, and Peter J. Casagrande, "Hardy's Wordsworth: A Record and a Commentary," *English Literature in Transition* 20 (1977), 212. See Gibson, 955, for the full note that accompanies the manuscript of "Domicilium" in the Dorset County Museum.

8. For a fuller description, see my "Hardy's Pocket Milton: An Early Unpublished Poem," *English Language Notes* XXV (March 1988), 49-52, and Dennis Taylor's "Hardy's Missing Poem and His Copy of Milton," *Thomas Hardy Journal* 6:1 (1990), 50-60.

9. Michale Millgate, *Thomas Hardy: A Biography* (New York: Random House, 1982), 89-90.

Appendix

Hardy's Mentors and Kinships, or How a Stonemason's Son Becomes a Poet

> *Thomas Hardy*
> *didn't like to party,*
> *but that posed no dilemma,*
> *since neither did Emma.*
> —Roberta Simone, "Clerihew Couples"

During the last thirty years of his life, Thomas Hardy was a revered but almost ghostly figure in English letters. Born in a rural backwater of England, in a village of a few cottages, the author of *The Return of the Native* returned to that rural county to build his house. The spot he chose was a lonely one, halfway between the village of his birth and the town where he had received his first sense of the wider world beyond Dorset. Unhappy in marriage, he increasingly lived in his upstairs study, leaving his wife Emma alone after meals in order to work on his writing or his correspondence. Though living a secluded life in his self-designed brick pile, Max Gate, he nevertheless received visitors, but with a polite reticence that was frequently remarked upon and that has been much parodied. Most could not imagine that the smallish man in an over-large coat who sat before them at tea was really the giant of English letters whose blessing they sought. He seemed quite ordinary. The photos of Hardy from this period show a quiet, somber, almost depressive man, frequently looking down. This image of him as the gloomy pessimist, reinforced by the fatalism of the novels and the melancholy of the poetry, has made it easy to see Hardy as not just a critic of Victorian society but as essentially outside of that society, someone preternaturally modern, someone who in some way prefigured the experiences of social disintegration and individual alienation so prevalent in the twentieth century. This view of Hardy which one gets from photographs, from his works, and from the reports of visitors, however, does not square at all with the whirl of social activity one finds in his chatty autobiography. There, with a dizzying dullness, Hardy records dinner parties, guest lists, seasons in London, visits to theaters, letters received, letters sent, conversations, invitations, honors, parades, titles, genealogies, gifts, speeches, all the social ephemera of his life. It seems that, in fact, Thomas Hardy did like to party. And so did his self-consciously middle-class wife Emma. But not with his family. The famous story that Emma required Hardy's mother to use the servant's entrance, true or untrue, strikes a chord because of Hardy's own ambivalent relationship to his roots. Hardy was extremely close to his mother and his sister Mary. He dutifully visited his parents on Sundays while they still lived. He seems to have especially enjoyed returning home at cider-making time, an activity which he presumably shared with his father and his brother, Henry. But few memories are recorded of any of them, or of his youngest sister, Kate. As his success in the literary world grew, his social and business life in London took him away from his family. Eventually, the family of writers he constructed for himself replaced his birth family altogether.

To even partially explore this thesis would require another book-length study, so I will only outline the story here. For the Hardy specialist, this will seem familiar ground. What is new is to realize that the nature of these relationships goes beyond the normal notions of friends, colleagues, acquaintances, and "influences." Their true nature is best understood by viewing them as a reconstructed family with extended kinship relationships.

Hardy's growth as an artist can be read as a story of removal and replacement. The first move, in early childhood, was away from his mother's knee and onto the lap of Julia Augusta Martin, wife of the local squire. In the primary school which she had founded, the young Hardy was introduced to the wider world that education brings. She also introduced him to the power of infatuation, to the consternation of his mother. Such strong feelings are the first intimations of the possibility of relating beyond the birth family and the beginning of the notion that one's true family might be somewhere else. In the words of William Stafford, one of the thoughts of the young child is "Maybe I'm a king" ("A Story That Could Be True").

Hardy's next removal, at age sixteen, was from Higher Bockhampton to the chief market town of the county, Dorchester, where he was apprenticed to an architect-builder, Mr. Hicks. Hardy's father and his stonemason's business were replaced by the higher aspirations of a professional career in architecture. In Dorchester, Hardy met a country parson and poet, William Barnes, and an older apprentice at Hicks's, Horace Moule, whose family members had been to university. Languages, literature, and learning were valued by these two in deeper ways than anyone he had yet known. With Moule and Barnes he formed strong mentoring relationships. Moule became like an older brother (Hardy was the firstborn in his family), teaching him Greek and choosing for him the books he ought to read. The learned yet rustic Barnes inspired him to think that a life of the mind was open to rural youths like him.

At the age of twenty-one, released from Hicks, Hardy received an offer of a journeyman's position in a prestigious London firm, A. W. Blomfield's. Blomfield was not only respectable but kind. There was a cheeriness and conviviality among the many apprentices and journeymen in his shop that led Hardy to regard him as the father of a large extended family, for which Hardy reverenced Blomfield all his life. Even more crucially, the removal from Dorchester to London put Hardy in the center of English intellectual life. His years there, from 1862 to 1867, were astonishingly rich. Hardy listened to T. H. Huxley debate the newly published ideas of Charles Darwin. He became a Darwinian and not a Christian. He attended plays weekly. He taught himself art history at the National Gallery. He studied in the British Museum's Reading Room. He talked and played and sang and danced and soaked in all that London, the center of the world, could offer. He decided to become a poet.

From whom could he learn to do this? Certainly not from his father, who knew about stonemasonry and cider-making. Certainly not from Hicks or Blomfield, who knew how to make him an architect. Moule was not a poet, but he had led Hardy to the poets. And these now became his family, replacing his father and subsequent father-figures. By this time Hardy had certainly read the Bible, the Greeks, Shakespeare, Byron, Scott, and even Dryden (in small pocket editions his mother had given him, still extant in the Dorset County Museum). These writers, to whom he would often allude later in his work, he seems to have accepted rather uncritically, as if he had found his heritage, his inheritance, and was only claiming what was there, not critiquing it. In later life, Hardy suggested that his very first poetry was Wordsworthian. But better evidence suggests that Hardy's first poet-mentor was Milton. It is Milton who stands as the great patriarch who initiated Hardy into the spiritual brotherhood of a muse-inspired life. The poetry he wrote during this period, however, failed. It did not arouse even a glimmer of interest in editors to whom Hardy sent it. He went back to Hicks, a junior architect now.

In his inner life, Hardy listened at the hall door to the great writers and thinkers of the past. They were distant relations at best, but at least he had a right to be in the house. In his practical working life, he was used by Hicks in the fastest growing segment of the business, the restoration of churches. On a business trip to the small parish of St. Juliot in distant Cornwall, Hardy fell under the charm of Arthurian legend associated with the spot and also under the charm of the clergyman's niece, Emma Gifford. She believed in him and in his potential to be a writer. Bolstered, Hardy set himself to trying his hand at novel-writing, on the grounds that, though less important than poetry, it was more practical, could earn him money, and allow them to marry. Now Hardy's mentors again shifted.

He was both lucky and unlucky in his initial choice of publishers. He sent his first attempt at a novel to Macmillan, and though it was rejected, Alexander Macmillan and his two readers, John Morley and George Meredith, took note of him, offering advice and encouragement. Morely's reader reports on Hardy's early efforts can still be read in the Macmillan Archives housed in the British Library. Macmillan rejected the next novel he sent them as well, but again offered encouragement, especially Meredith. Later, Hardy found the editor of *Cornhill Magazine*, Leslie Stephen, to be a useful teacher and lifelong friend. Meredith's view of the novel and Stephen's editing practices were initiatory influences in Hardy's second career, as the architect was displaced by the novelist. Meredith and Stephens functioned as mentoring Dutch uncles for him.

During this period of growing literary success, Hardy experienced jealousies and sibling rivalries with other practicing novelists, with George Moore, G. K. Chesterton, and Henry James, most notably. Some of the bitterness of those feelings can be seen in his dictated deathbed diatribes on Moore and Chesterton, and in the aspersions in his autobiography cast upon James's "manliness," who had defamed Hardy's own by naming him "Little Thomas Hardy." Rudyard Kipling, Edmund Gosse, James Barrie, and Arthur Symons he regarded more affectionately, almost as younger brothers. When he turned from novels to poetry in the late 1890s, however, Hardy needed yet another set of mentors, and experienced a new set of jealousies. This time, at nearly sixty, he seems not to have turned to anyone living, but to have taken on his nineteenth-century predecessors, as both fathers and rivals. Of the Romantics, he loved Shelley the best and fought the most with Wordsworth. Of his nearer masters, Swinburne was the most admired and uncritically digested; Tennyson, Arnold, and Browning were acknowledged, even loved in the case of Browning, but ultimately rejected.

During this third career, as a poet, Hardy measured himself against a tradition. He kept track of changing poetic ideals, reading widely, including Pound and Eliot, but his poetry seemed from a different time. Younger writers treated him as a kindly patriarch, a literary godfather whom they wanted to honor and from whom they wanted just a word, a blessing. These literary grandchildren included Leslie Stephen's daughter, Virginia Woolf, and Robert Bridges' daughter, Elizabeth Daryush; older poets such as Edward Thomas, Robert Frost, and W. B. Yeats; the younger Georgians such as Robert Graves, Siegfried Sassoon, and T. E. Lawrence; and a generation too young to have visited him, W. H. Auden, John Betjeman, and C. Day Lewis.

Some of the literary kinships mentioned so far had the intensity one would expect in true family relationships. There are passionate and difficult relationships with fathers and brothers, for example. But one wonders—where are the mothers, sisters, wives, sons, and daughters? The issue of mothers has been widely addressed in its general form by feminist critics. What woman, what foremother stands firmly enough on the horizon to act as a guiding influence? What is the female tradition as Hardy could have known it? It is from the female, from his mother, that Hardy learned to read, and through her that he received his first books, but apart from Sappho there is mostly silence. The question of sisters is complicated by the realities of the nineteenth-century literary marketplace. The early reviews of Hardy's second published novel, *Under the Greenwood Tree*, speculated that it was written by George Eliot, which bothered Hardy enormously. He was at great pains to join with Kipling in the "society of virile authors," to distance himself from the "lady novelists" of the day. One might speculate that for one of Hardy's family background, literature and writing were the province of the female, his mother and his sister Mary (training to be a schoolteacher), and that to maintain his identity and his masculinity he would not consciously look to literary sisters or mothers, even if there had been a rich and available tradition.

As for wives and lovers, Hardy had many and he had none. He was married, of course, twice, first to Emma Gifford for almost forty years and then after her death to Florence Dugdale. He carried on lifelong infatuations, sometimes based on nothing more than a smile from a girl passing him in the lane when he was a boy. Sometimes the flirtations were more actively pursued, most notably with Mrs. Florence Henniker during his marriage to Emma, and during his second marriage with a local girl, Gertrude Bugler, whom he picked to play the part of Tess in a dramatic version of his most famous novel. In each of these relationships he saw his partner as a literary or theatrical collaborator. Emma and both Florences had literary pretensions which he at first encouraged and then regretted. None of the partnerships was ultimately enriching for him, literarily or personally. He worked and lived alone.

Children were the most disappointing of all. Hardy had none. It seems to be one of the difficulties in his relationship with Emma, a sadness and emptiness that led him further from her rather than closer to her. Literarily, however, it might be argued that he did have children. Certainly all those writers whom I have named grandchildren almost clamored for his blessing, or spoke of him whom they never had met in affectionately reverent tones, as Philip Larkin did. These relationships seem more distant, however, than that between parents and children, nearer to the relationship that Hardy was able to construct with the great patriarchs of English poetry, Milton and Shakespeare. Just as he was able to accept them rather uncritically as his birthright, so the Georgians and the Movement poets of later years could look to Hardy as an anchor to the past who could be honored if not exactly obeyed in all the fine details of making poems. But two poets have a greater claim to the status of son and daughter than any of these.

The son, arguably, is D. H. Lawrence, who had to write a tortured *Study of Thomas Hardy* to work Hardy out of his system. Lawrence, who could not learn novel-writing from his own coal-miner father, may have been attracted to the similar class difficulties Hardy faced in not coming from the middle class. Lawrence defined Hardy as a great novelist who was ultimately wrong, someone who had to be taken on and rebelled against. That is, Lawrence treated Hardy as Hardy treated Wordsworth. Lawrence's poetry both derives from Hardy and rejects it. As with his father-poet, any topic under the sun is fair game, and so is any chosen awkwardness, any honoring of dialect, any forbidden idea. At the same time, the old forms of the father are completely dashed and broken, the poetry of the past abandoned for "the poetry of the present."

The daughter is Charlotte Mew. Hardy was astounded when he first read Mew's *The Farmer's Bride*. He called her the best living female poet. Those qualifiers were mocked by Virginia Woolf, among others, who saw her as Thomas Hardy's "favorite poetess." For Hardy, however, who recognized no ancestral or contemporary female voices more recent than Sappho, the phrasing of his praise meant that here was the first woman poet. During her life, he worked diligently to secure her a pension from the Civil List, providing her a living so that she could devote herself to poetry. After her death, his praise has provoked a reevaluation of her work. The passionate, quirky, sometimes macabre work of the father is carried on and advanced by the true daughter.

Hardy's descendents are so various that they hardly seem to belong at the same family reunion—Welsh poets Dylan Thomas and Vernon Watkins, the Scots Edwin Muir and Andrew Young, the Movement's Donald Davie and Philip Larkin, Belfast poets Tom Paulin and Seamus Heaney, establishment poets Andrew Motion and Anthony Thwaite, workingclass-identified Tony Harrison, and overseas-born Fleur Adcock. Perhaps the metaphor is rather of a public funeral or banquet at which those who loved the deceased pay their respects and offer toasts that indicate he is still in the minds of the living, if not always exactly evident in their poetry. Hardy's influence seems to come from the example of a long writing life more than from any particular work, talent, or technique. He gives permission for any life, with whatever poor or rich materials it finds at hand, to be transformed by art.

Bibliography

Aarsleff, Hans. *From Locke to Saussure: Essays on the Study of Language and Intellectual History*. Minneapolis: University of Minnesota Press, 1982.

———. "Language and Victorian Ideology." *The American Scholar* (Summer 1983), 365-72.

———. *The Study of Language in England 1780-1860*. Princeton, N.J.: Princeton University Press, 1967.

Archer, William. *Real Conversations*. London: Heinemann, 1904.

Armstrong, Isobel. *Language As Living Form in Nineteenth Century Poetry*. Totowa, N.J.: Barnes & Noble, 1982.

———. *Victorian Poetry: Poetry, Poetics, Politics*. London: Routledge, 1993.

Auden, W. H. "A Literary Transference." *Southern Review* 6 (1940), 78-86.

Bailey, J. O. *The Poetry of Thomas Hardy: A Handbook and Commentary*. Chapel Hill: University of North Carolina Press, 1970.

Barnes, William. *William Barnes, the Dorset Poet: A Comprehensive Selection of Poetry and Prose*. Ed. and sel. Chris Wrigley. Stanbridge, Wimborne, Dorset: Dovecote Press, 1984.

Beer, Gillian. *Darwin's Plots: Evolutionary Narrative in Darwin, George Eliot, and Nineteenth Century Fiction*. London: Routledge & Kegan Paul, 1983.

Bennett, Joan. "An Aspect of the Evolution of Nineteenth Century Prose," *Review of English Studies*, 17 (1941), 281-97.

Benzie, William. *Dr. F. J. Furnivall: A Victorian Scholar Adventurer*. Norman, Okla.: Pilgrim Books, 1983.

Berger, Sheila. *Thomas Hardy and Visual Structures: Framing, Disruption, Process*. New York: New York University Press, 1990.

Black, Max. *Models and Metaphors: Studies in Language and Philosophy*. Ithaca, N.Y.: Cornell University Press, 1962.

Bloom, Harold. *The Anxiety of Influence: A Theory of Poetry*. Oxford: Oxford University Press, 1973.

———. *A Map of Misreading*. Oxford: Oxford University Press, 1975.

———. ed. *Thomas Hardy: Modern Critical Views*. New York: Chelsea House, 1987.

Browning, Robert. *Robert Browning: The Poems*. Eds. John Pettigrew and Thomas J. Collins. 2 vols. New Haven, Conn.: Yale University Press, 1981.
Bruns, Gerald. *Modern Poetry and the Idea of Language*. New Haven, Conn.: Yale University Press, 1974.
Buckler, William E. *The Poetry of Thomas Hardy: A Study in Art and Ideas*. New York: New York University Press, 1983.
Burkhardt, Frederick, ed. *Charles Darwin's Letters: A Selection*. Cambridge: Cambridge University Press, 1996.
Burtt, E. A. *The Metaphysical Foundations of Modern Science*. 1955. Reprint, New York: Doubleday-Anchor, 1930.
Butler, Lance St. John. *Thomas Hardy after Fifty Years*. Totowa, N.J.: Rowman & Littlefield, 1977.
Casagrande, Peter J. *Hardy's Influence on the Modern Novel*. Totowa, N.J.: Barnes & Noble, 1987.
———. "Hardy's Wordsworth: A Record and a Commentary." *English Literature in Transition* 20 (1977), 210-37.
———. *Unity in Hardy's Novels*. Lawrence: Regents Press of Kansas, 1982.
Chapmen, Raymond. *The Language of Thomas Hardy*. New York: St. Martin's, 1990.
Christ, Carol T. *The Finer Optic*. New Haven, Conn.: Yale University Press, 1975.
Christ, Carol T. and John O. Jordan, eds. *Victorian Literature and the Victorian Visual Imagination*. Berkeley: University of California Press, 1995.
Collins, Deborah L. *Thomas Hardy and His God: A Liturgy of Unbelief*. New York: St. Martin's Press, 1990.
Dale, Peter Allan. "'Gracious Lies': The Meaning of Metaphor in *In Memoriam*." *Victorian Poetry* 2 (1980), 147-67.
Darwin, Charles. *The Autobiography of Charles Darwin*. Ed. Francis Darwin. 1892. Reprint, New York: Dover, 1958.
———. *The Origin of Species*. Ed. Gillian Beer. Oxford: Oxford University Press, 1996.
Davie, Donald. *Thomas Hardy and British Poetry*. New York: Oxford University Press, 1972.
Desmond, Adrian. *Huxley: From Devil's Disciple to Evolution's High Priest*. Reading, Mass.: Addison-Wesley, 1994.
Desmond, Adrian, and James Moore. *Darwin: The Life of a Tormented Evolutionist*. New York: Warner, 1991.
Dreger, Alice. *Hermaphrodites and the Medical Invention of Sex*. Cambridge, Mass.: Harvard University Press, 1998.
Ebbatson, Roger. *The Evolutionary Self*. Totowa, N.J.: Barnes & Noble, 1982.
Gillespie, Charles Coulston. *The Edge of Objectivity*. Princeton: Princeton University Press, 1960.
Gittings, Robert. *Young Thomas Hardy*. Boston: Little, Brown, 1975.

———. *The Older Hardy*. London: Heinemann, 1979.
Green, Brian. *Hardy's Lyrics: Pearls of Pity*. London: Macmillan, 1996.
Gridley, Roy. *Browning*. Boston: Routledge & Kegan Paul, 1972.
———. *The Brownings and France: A Chronicle with Commentary*. London: Athlone Press, 1982.
Grundy, Joan. *Hardy and the Sister Arts*. London: Macmillan, 1979.
Hardy, Emma. *Emma Hardy Diaries*, ed. Richard H. Taylor. Manchester: Mid Northumberland Arts Group and Carcanet New Press, 1985.
Hardy, Evelyn. *Thomas Hardy: A Critical Biography*. New York: Russell & Russell, 1954.
Hardy, Thomas. *The Collected Letters of Thomas Hardy*, ed. Richard Purdy and Michael Millgate. 7 vols. Oxford: Oxford University Press, 1978-1988.
———. *The Complete Poems of Thomas Hardy*. Ed. James Gibson. London: Macmillan, 1976.
———. *The Complete Poetical Works of Thomas Hardy*. Ed. Samuel Hynes. 3 vols. Oxford: Oxford University Press, 1982-1985.
———. *The Early Life of Thomas Hardy, 1840-1891* (nominally by Florence Emily Hardy). New York: Macmillan, 1928.
———. *The Later Years of Thomas Hardy, 1892-1928* (nominally by Florence Emily Hardy). New York: Macmillan, 1930.
———. *The Life and Work of Thomas Hardy*. Ed. Michael Millgate. London: Macmillan, 1985.
———. *The Literary Notebooks of Thomas Hardy*. Ed. Lennart A. Bjork. 2 vols. London: Macmillan, 1985.
———. *The Personal Notebooks of Thomas Hardy*. Ed. Richard H. Taylor. New York: Columbia University Press, 1979.
———. *Personal Writings: Prefaces, Literary Opinions, Reminiscenses*. Ed. Harold Orel. Lawrence: University of Kansas Press, 1966.
———. *Thomas Hardy: Interviews and Recollections*. Ed. James Gibson. London: Macmillan, 1999.
———. *The Variorum Edition of the Complete Poems of Thomas Hardy*. Ed. James Gibson. New York: Macmillan, 1978.
Harris, Wendell V. *The Omnipresent Debate*. DeKalb: Northern Illinois University Press, 1981.
Hawkes, Terence. *Metaphor*. Bristol, U.K.: J. W. Arrowsmith, 1972.
Hynes, Samuel. *The Pattern of Hardy's Poetry*. Chapel Hill: University of North Carolina Press, 1961.
Jacobs, Willis D. *William Barnes, Linguist*. Albuquerque: University of New Mexico Press, 1952.
Johnson, Mark, ed. *Philosophical Perspectives on Metaphor*. Minneapolis: University of Minnesota Press, 1981.
Jones, Keith W. J. *The Poetry of Nature: Rural Perspectives in Poetry from Wordsworth to the Present*. Toronto: University of Toronto Press, 1980.
Kramer, Dale, ed. *The Cambridge Companion to Thomas Hardy*. Cambridge: Cambridge University Press, 1999.

Kuhn, Thomas S. *The Structure of Scientific Revolutions*. 2nd ed. 1970: University of Chicago Press, 1962.

Lakoff, George, and Mark Johnson. *Metaphors We Live By*. Chicago: University of Chicago Press, 1980.

———. *Philosophy in the Flesh: The Embodied Mind and Its Challenge to Western Thought*. New York: Basic Books, 1999.

Langbaum, Robert. *The Poetry of Experience*. New York: Norton, 1957.

———. *Thomas Hardy in Our Time*. London: Macmillan, 1995.

Laqueur, Thomas. *Making Sex: Body and Gender from the Greeks to Freud*. Cambridge, Mass.: Harvard University Press, 1992.

Larkin, Philip. "Wanted: Good Hardy Critic." *Critical Quarterly* 8 (1966), 174-79.

Lawrence, David Herbert. "Study of Thomas Hardy." *Phoenix: The Posthumous Papers of D. H. Lawrence*. Ed. Edward D. MacDonald. New York: Viking, 1936.

Lea, Hermann. *Thomas Hardy: Through the Camera's Eye*. Beaminster, Dorset: The Toucan Press, 1964.

Leavis, F. R. "Hardy the Poet." *Southern Review* 6 (1940), 87-98.

Lewis, Cecil Day. "The Lyrical Poetry of Thomas Hardy." *Proceedings of the British Academy*, 37, 1951.

Marsden, Kenneth. *The Poems of Thomas Hardy: A Critical Introduction*. New York: Oxford University Press, 1969.

Mason, Michael. *The Making of Victorian Sexuality*. Oxford: Oxford University Press, 1994.

Maynard, Katerine Kearney. *Thomas Hardy's Tragic Poetry: The Lyrics and the Dynasts*. Iowa City: University of Iowa Press, 1991.

Miller, J. Hillis. *Thomas Hardy: Distance and Desire*. Cambridge, Mass.: Harvard University Press, 1970.

Millgate, Michael. *Thomas Hardy, a Biography*. New York: Oxford University Press, 1982.

———. *Testamentary Acts: Browning, Tennyson, James, Hardy*. Oxford: Clarendon Press, 1992.

Montefiore, Jan. *Feminism and Poetry: Language, Experience, Identity in Women's Writing*. 2nd ed. London: Harper Collins, 1994.

Mugglestone, Lynda. *"Talking Proper": The Rise of Accent as Social Symbol*. Oxford: Clarendon, 1995.

Murfin, Ross C. *Swinburne, Hardy, Lawrence and the Burden of Belief*. Chicago: University of Chicago Press. 1978.

Orel, Harold, ed. *Critical Essays on Thomas Hardy's Poetry*. New York: G. K. Hall, 1995.

———. *The Final Years of Thomas Hardy, 1912-1928*. Lawrence: University of Kansas Press, 1976.

Page, Norman. *Thomas Hardy*. London: Routledge and Kegan Paul, 1977.

———. *Thomas Hardy Annual*. Nos. 1-5. London: Humanities Press/ Macmillan, 1983-1987.

———. *Thomas Hardy: The Writer and his Background.* New York: St. Martin's Press, 1980.
Paulin, Tom. *Thomas Hardy: The Poetry of Perception.* Totowa, N.J.: Rowman & Littlefield, 1975.
Persoon, James. "'A Sign-Seeker' and 'Cleon': Hardy's Argument with Browning." *Victorian Newsletter* (Fall 1998), 32-36.
———. "'Dover Beach,' Hardy's Version." *Critical Essays on Thomas Hardy's Poetry.* Ed. Harold Orel. New York: G. K. Hall, 1995.
———. *Modern British Poetry, 1900-1939.* New York: Twayne, 1999.
———. "Hardy's Pocket Milton." *English Language Notes* (March 1988), 49-52.
———. "Once More to 'The Darkling Thrush': Hardy's Reversals of Milton." *CEA Critic* (Summer/Fall 1986), 76-86.
Pettit, Charles P. C., ed. *Celebrating Thomas Hardy.* London: Macmillan, 1996.
Pinion, F. B. *A Commentary on the Poems of Thomas Hardy.* London: Macmillan, 1976.
———. *A Hardy Companion.* London: Macmillan, 1968.
———. *Thomas Hardy: His Life and Friends.* New York: St. Martin's, 1992.
Purdy, Richard Little. *Thomas Hardy: A Bibliographical Study.* Oxford: Clarendon Press, 1954.
Ralling, Christopher. *The Voyage of Charles Darwin: Autobiographical Writings.* New York: Mayflower, 1979.
Ransom, John Crowe. "Honey and Gall." *Southern Review* 6 (1940).
———. *Selected Poems of Thomas Hardy.* New York: Macmillan, 1960.
Reed, John R. *Victorian Conventions.* Columbus: Ohio University Press, 1975.
Robertson, D. W. *A Preface to Chaucer.* Princeton: Princeton University Press, 1962.
Roszak, Theodore. "Away with Miracles and Meanings." *Book World* (October 24, 1971), 16.
Rothenstein, William. *Men and Memories: Recollections of William Rothenstein, 1872-1900.* New York: Coward-McCann, 1931.
Salter, C. H. "Unusual Words Beginning with *un, en, out, up* and *on* in Thomas Hardy's Verse." *Victorian Poetry* 11 (1973), 257-61.
Schur, Owen. *Victorian Pastoral: Tennyson, Hardy, and the Subversion of Forms.* Columbus: Ohio State University Press, 1989.
Seymour-Smith, Martin. *Hardy.* London: Bloomsbury, 1994.
Springer, Marlene. *Hardy's Use of Allusion.* Lawrence: University Press of Kansas, 1983.
Stave, Shirley A. *The Decline of the Goddess: Nature, Culture, and Women in Thomas Hardy's Fiction.* London: Greenwood Press, 1995.
Sussman, Herbert. *Victorians and the Machine.* Cambridge, Mass.: Harvard University Press, 1968.
Tate, Allen. "Hardy's Philosophic Metaphors." *Southern Review* 6 (1940), 99-110.

Taylor, Dennis E. "The Chronology of Hardy's Poetry." *Victorian Poetry* 37:1 (Spring 1999), 1-57.

———. "Hardy's Copy of Tennyson's *In Memoriam*." *Thomas Hardy Journal* 13 (February 1997), 43-63.

———. *Hardy's Literary Language and Victorian Philology*. Oxford: Clarendon Press, 1993.

———. *Hardy's Metres and Victorian Prosody*. Oxford: Clarendon Press, 1988.

———. "Hardy's Missing poem and his Copy of Milton." *Thomas Hardy Journal* 6 (February 1990), 50-60.

———. *Hardy's Poetry, 1860-1928*. New York: Columbia University Press, 1981.

Taylor, Jenny Bourne, and Sally Shuttleworth, eds. *Embodied Selves: An Anthology of Psychological Texts, 1830-1890*. Oxford: Clarendon Press, 1998.

Tennyson, Alfred Lord. *In Memoriam*. 1850. Ed. Robert Ross. New York: Norton, 1973.

Thomas, Alan. *The Expanding Eye: Photography and the 19th Century Mind*. London: Croom Helm, 1978.

Trench, Richard Chenevix. *On the Study of Words*. 1851. Reprint, 18th ed. New York: Macmillan, n.d.

———. *Poems*. 8th ed. London: Macmillan, 1879.

Turbayne, Colin. *The Myth of Metaphor*. Rev. ed. Columbia: University of South Carolina Press, 1970.

Turner, Paul. *The Life of Thomas Hardy: A Critical Biography*. London: Blackwell, 1998.

Wallace, Anne D. *Walking, Literature, and English Culture: The Origins and Uses of the Peripatetic in the Nineteenth Century*. Oxford: Clarendon Press, 1993.

Willey, Basil. *The Religion of Nature*. London: The Lindsey Press, 1957.

———. *The Seventeenth Century Background*. 1935. Reprint, New York: Anchor, 1953.

Zietlow, Paul. *Moments of Vision: The Poetry of Thomas Hardy*. Cambridge, Mass.: Harvard University Press, 1974.

Index

Aarsleff, Hans, 48
Antoinette, Marie, 29
Archer, William, 70, 71
Archilochus, 1
Armstrong, Isobel, 2
Armstrong, Tim, 6
Auden, W. H., 48
Augustine, 59

Bacon, Francis, 49-50
Bailey, J. O., 7, 40
Barnes, William, 47, 52-54
Bentham, Jeremy, 50-51
Benvenuto, Richard, 73-74
Berlin, Isaiah, 1
Betjeman, John, 77
Bjork, Lennart, 88
Blomfield, Sir Arthur, 18, 95
Bloom, Harold, 1, 80
Bly, Robert, 67
Browning, Robert, 7, 10-11; "Cleon," 7-11; *The Ring and the Book*, 10; "La Saisaiz," 11

Carlyle, Thomas, 67
Casagrande, Peter, 1, 17, 44, 81
Chaucer, Geoffrey, 48, 59
Cixous, Helene, 32
Coleridge, Samuel Taylor, 62n5, 68

Daguerre, Louis-Jacques Mande, 60

Daiches, David, 1, 74
Darwin, Charles, 5, 18, 51, 52, 60, 95
Dawkins, Richard, 78
Davie, Donald, 72, 77
Delaroche, Paul, 60
dualism, 2-3, 14, 19, 33, 44-45

Eliot, T. S., 47, 84
empiricism, 12-14, 50-51
etymology, in the nineteenth century, 52, 53, 59-60

Genesis, 49
Georgianism, 87-88
Gibson, James, 82-83
Gosse, Sir Edmund, 17, 18-19, 34n4
Graves, Robert, 79, 81

Hall, Donald, 75
Hardy, Emma, 88, 93, 94
Hardy, Florence, 5
Hardy, Thomas:
"Apology" to *Late Lyrics and Earlier*, 26, 70, 72-73; "bilberry eye" of, 2; *Desperate Remedies*, 44-45; "The Dorsetshire Labourer," 38; *The Dynasts*, 29, 87; female speakers in, 44-45; *Jude the Obscure*, 13, 71, 80; and loving-kindness, 26, 72, 74;

"Memories of Church Restoration," 54-58, 61; Mother Nature in, 26, 32; poems, individual: "Ah, Are You Digging on My Grave," 38-39; "Amabel," 24-25; "At a Lunar Eclipse," 70; "At the Railway Station, Upway," 76; "A Broken Appointment," 74; "The Caged Goldfinch," 71; "The Caged Thrush Freed and Home Again," 71; "Channel Firing," 87; "The Convergence of the Twain," 87; "A Daughter Returns," 28; "The Darkling Thrush," 72; "Discouragement," 26; "Domicilium," 17, 18, 81-82; "Dream of the City Shopwoman," 28-30; "Epitaph by Labourers," 82; "From Her in the Country," 28-30; "The Gap in the White," 74, 88-89; "The Going," 88; "Going and Staying," 71; "Hap," 24, 25, 63-64, 67; "Haunting Fingers," 69; "He Abjures Love," 20-21; "He Resolves to Say No More," 72; "Heiress and Architect," 30; "Her Confession," 41-42; "Her Definition," 19, 20; "Her Dilemma," 22-23, 31, 74; "Her Immortality," 38-39; "Her Reproach," 42-43; "A Hurried Meeting," 74; "I Look into My Glass," 70; "The Impercipient at a Cathedral Service," 45; "In St. Paul's a While Ago," 7; "In Vision I Roamed," 25-26, 67; "Jubilate," 68-69; "The Last Chrysanthemum," 73-74; "Let Me Enjoy," 66-67; "The Minute Before Meeting," 41; "Nature's Questioning," 63; "Neutral Tones," 83, 84-87; "1967," 19-20; "Proud Songsters," 75-76; "Retty's Phases," 83; "Revulsion," 30-31; "The Ruined Maid," 28; "She at His Funeral," 43; "She, to Him" sonnets, 37, 39-41; "The Sick Battle-God," 80; "A Sign-Seeker," 8-11; "Tess's Lament," 23-24; "To an Actress," 19, 20; "To an Impersonator of Rosalind," 19, 20; "The Two Houses," 70; "The Two Rosalinds," 27; "A Young Man's Epigram on Existence," 31-32; "A Young Man's Exhortation," 27-28; "We Are Getting to the End," 71-72; "Weathers," 76-77; poetry, dating of, 17-18, 80, 81-83; photography, views on, 60; *Tess of the d'Urbervilles*, 71; *Wessex Poems*, 18, 34n3, 83, 84, 87

Heaney, Seamus, 78
Hobbes, Thomas, 50
Horace, 24-25
Hughes, Ted, 73; "Crow's Account of the Battle," 73
Hulme, T. E., 84, 88
Hynes, Samuel, 1, 71

imagism, 87-88

Johnson, Mark, 65-66

Lakoff, George, 65-66
Langbaum, Robert, 2, 6, 88
Larkin, Philip, vii, 47, 77-78; "High Windows," 63
Lawrence, D. H., 72, 73, 98
Lea, Hermann, 12, 81
Leavis, F. R., 47, 61n1
Lerner, Laurence, 2
Locke, John, 31, 50, 62n5, 66

Lucas, John, 34n3, 72

Marsh, Edward, 88
Martin, Julia Augusta, 94
Meredith, George, 96
Mew, Charlotte, 98-99
Mill, John Stuart, 5
Miller, J. Hillis, 1, 34n4
Millgate, Michael, 82
Milton, John, 48, 82
modernism, 84, 87
Monod, Jacques, 64
Montefiore, Jan, 32
Morley, John, 96

Paulin, Tom, 1, 5, 8-9, 21, 74-75
pessimism, 5, 33, 72-74
photography, as art, 60
Pound, Ezra, 80, 84, 88, 89, 91n6

Ransom, John Crowe, 1, 77
Roszak, Theodore, 64
Rothenstein, Sir William, 2
Ruskin, John, 5

sacramentalism, 48-49, 50, 61, 64-65
Shelley, Percy Bysshe, 6, 51; *A Defense of Poetry*, 51

Sickert, Walter Richard, 85
Skeat, W. W., 52
Stafford, William, 94; "A Story That Could Be True," 94
Stephen, Leslie, 7
Strachey, Lytton, 47
Swift, Jonathan, 50
symbolism, 84, 87
Symons, Arthur, 84-87; "Gray and Green," 85-86

Tate, Allen, 63
Taylor, Dennis, 10, 48, 51
Tennyson, Alfred, Lord, 8-10; *In Memoriam*, 8-10; "Locksley Hall," 8
Thackeray, Anne (Lady Ritchie), 7
Tolstoy, Leo, 1
Tooke, John Horne, 52
Trench, Richard Chenevix, 51-52
Turner, Paul, 24-25

Van Gogh, Vincent, 60

Wordsworth, William, 6, 51, 62n5, 81-82; "Tintern Abbey," 21

Yeats, William Butler, 78, 87

About the Author

James Persoon is currently a professor of English at Grand Valley State University, Allendale, Michigan, where he has directed several of its writing programs. He has published articles and notes on Arnold, Browning, Hardy, Shelley, Shakespeare, Milton, Orwell, and Kipling, and is the author of *Modern British Poetry 1900-1939* (Twayne, 1999). In 1990 he was the English tutor for the Post-Graduate-Certificate-in-Education course at the University of Newcastle-upon-Tyne. He resides in Grand Haven, Michigan, with his wife, the fiction writer Christl Reges, and with the remaining adolescents among their six children.